CONGRATULATIONS GRADUATE!

You believed you could – and you did!

Remember that the most incredible achievements started with someone dreaming big, believing they could do it, and pursuing it relentlessly. So, keep believing that you can, even when your dreams seem crazy to others.

Don't be discouraged by setbacks, failures, or naysayers. Instead, let that be what inspires you to take action–to challenge the impossible. You are persistent, resilient, and adaptable.

The world needs dreamers like you with a willingness to pursue your passions and use them to make the world a better place. Christopher Newport taught you to lead a life of significance and now we're counting on you to continue to dream big, to believe in yourself, and to make a difference.

You've got this.

GO CAPTAINS!

THE STORY OF THE TRANSFORMATION
OF CHRISTOPHER NEWPORT UNIVERSITY

CRAZY
AS
HELL

Library of Congress Cataloging-in-Publication Data is available upon request.

Jacket and Book Design – Katie Bishop
Art Direction and Production Management – Amie Dale

All photographs courtesy of Christopher Newport Office of Communication and Public Relations, the Trible Library Archive and Amanda Robbins Photography

Boyd's Eye View Comic reprinted with permission from Bentley Boyd

ISBN 9780578361338 (paperback)
ISBN 9780578361345 (ebook)

Published by IngramSpark

THE STORY OF THE TRANSFORMATION
OF CHRISTOPHER NEWPORT UNIVERSITY

CRAZY

AS

HELL

ELLEN VAUGHN

TABLE OF CONTENTS

To Paul and Rosemary Trible,
who began
with the end in mind

President Paul Trible addresses graduating students at the Senior Gift Toast during Commencement Week with his faithful companion Bella Trible at his side.

CHAPTER 1

BEGINNINGS

"Where there's life there's hope, and need of vittles."
— *J.R.R. TOLKIEN, THE LORD OF THE RINGS*

F or first-year students at Virginia's Christopher Newport University, the journey often begins with peanut butter pie. After bidding farewell to their parents and getting settled in their residence halls, each of the 1,200 new students considers his or her invitation to spend an evening at the home of the university president and his wife. RSVPs are required, as well as business attire.

The guests are invited in batches of several hundred, on succeeding evenings. The President's home, owned by the university and a mile from campus, can accommodate such numbers. Most of the new students choose to come.

They arrive in tidy white vans organized by the office of university events. Some of the vans are a bit quiet, as some of the young people are feeling homesick, or awkward, or tired. Many raise their eyebrows as the vans turn into the long circular drive that leads to the gracious entrance of The Three Oaks, a red-brick, waterfront Georgian home with its symmetrical wings, white columns, and slender chimneys for the four fireplaces.

President Paul Trible stands on the semicircle front porch, impeccably turned out in his customary blue pinstripe suit, Ledbury shirt with French cuffs and gold cufflinks, bright red tie, tassel loafers, and United States Senate ring. He is effusive, comfortable in his well-cut clothes and in his own skin, and jovial.

"Welcome to our home!" he calls to students before they even ascend the brick stairs. "We are so glad you're here!"

A nervous 18-year-old student from a rural county in Virginia has somehow been pushed to be first in line. "I'm Paul Trible," says his host. "Welcome!"

"I'm John," the student replies, looking down.

"John who?" Paul responds, shaking his hand. "Tell me your last name. Where are you from?"

Paul Trible greets each guest, pats their shoulders, looks into their eyes, asks questions, He is genuinely interested and hospitably flawless. It's as if he's an old politician.

The students make their way into the warm home. Its ceilings soar. There is a sweeping mahogany staircase, marble floors, chandeliers, rich wallpaper, enormous sprays of flowers, and the smiling faces of a few upper-class students, faculty, and staff welcoming the guests further in. There is a massive great room with fireplaces at either end, stone mantels, overstuffed chairs, framed family photos, and tall, arched windows that look out to a bricked porch and a green lawn, marked by three perfect 100-year-old trees. The willow oaks guard the James River, five miles wide at this point, the same James River where a daring young Captain Christopher Newport commanded a fleet of three ships bringing the first settlers to Jamestown in the spring of 1607.

As the students enter the great room, they are greeted by a miniature force of nature, one Rosemary Trible. Rosemary, married to Paul Trible since 1971, is a diminutive woman whose mighty spirit overflows with enthusiasm, affection, compassion, and connection. She hugs, welcomes, and directs students to help themselves to something to drink and then make their way outside.

Near Rosemary's feet is the third member of the welcoming family. The dog. For years it was a golden retriever named Mollie I, followed by Mollie II, then an equally beautiful golden named Bella, who considers herself the first lady of CNU.

Many of the kids miss their dogs, left behind when they went off to college. They crowd around Bella, petting her warm gold fur, speaking to her in dog language. Her tail thumps against the students' legs as she welcomes each one.

Already, many young people who arrived a bit stiff, clutching their cell phones, are relaxed, going with the easy flow.

Eventually everyone gathers outside on the massive green lawn, which is studded with round standup tables draped with crisp white linens and topped with small candles. The sun is sinking above the James; the sunset is going to be extraordinary.

Paul and Rosemary, whose smooth choreography of the evening is well rehearsed, take their places under the portico, speaking to the array of students from the top of the steps there.

Paul wants the students to know that they are beginning what can be the best four years of their lives. He tells them they've arrived at a unique university, that they are part of a community of caring, excellence, and beauty.

Many of the students nod. Their parents went crazy when they originally toured this shiny school. During Paul Trible's presidency, more than a billion dollars' worth of capital improvements have gone into the campus. The buildings are massive, gorgeous, and pristine, with golden cupolas, arches, courtyards, a bell tower, and modern glass structures paired with enormous, red-brick classic edifices. The grass is perfectly green, every blade standing at attention, yet somehow soft to bare feet when students throw frisbees on the Great Lawn. There are flowers and graceful plantings everywhere. The residence halls have fireplaces, lounges, and comfortable suites. The library soars with 1.2 million volumes and innovative technology. The blue and white football stadium rocks. There is every club or activity one could think of. Upper class students routinely hold doors open for you. The coffee is always hot, the food is extraordinary, and smiling Miss Linda and Miss Virginia in the dining hall are legends. Everything is polished, clean, and perfect. Some students have said it's like Disney World.

Paul Trible now asks members of the faculty to introduce themselves, staccato fashion. Here's the head of philosophy and religion department, with his ponytail and quick laugh. Here's the Provost, an Ivy-league physicist with a luxuriant mustache that defies the laws of gravity. Here's the irrepressible Director of Music, a brass musician and conductor who has never met a stranger. Here is the Dean of Arts and Humanities in her navy suit and strand of pearls. She's an internationally acclaimed expert on Immanuel Kant, who smiles and makes students feel like they *can*.

They all say a few words, crack jokes, and invite the first-year students to talk with them tonight or come see them any time. Their doors, like President Trible's, are always open to students.

The young men and women crane their necks, getting a better look at this professor or that faculty member, noting who they want to talk with later.

For her part, Rosemary Trible tells the students she has led a women's Bible discussion group in her home once a week for the last few decades. Any young women who might be interested are welcome to come.

She also directs the students to the dessert table. They have not eaten since dinner, an hour or two ago, and are starving. Rosemary hands glass plates to each student, inviting them to sample cheesecakes, key lime pies, Heath Bar crunch pies, chocolate layer creations, and the confection that has already made a buzz on the student grapevine: peanut butter pie. It's about a foot tall, chilled on a crunchy Oreo crust with mounds of chocolate, peanut butter, cream cheese, nuts, and a whipped cream garnish.

The students crunch pie, sip drinks, and circulate. They talk with professors; they connect with one another. The sunset is glorious. Rays of scarlet and gold light the sky like sustained fireworks over the James' quiet blue waters.

As they leave, an impromptu line forms. Most of the students wants selfies with the Tribles; everyone wants a photo with the dog. They laugh. Most hug the Tribles and each other. They get each other's contact information as they crowd into the noisy white vans to head back to campus. They have begun to get the idea that in fact they are part of a family.

Statistics are hard to come by, but it appears that presidents of public universities in the United States have an average tenure of about five years. Some higher education observers have noted a "revolving door" tendency in such positions, which can lead to constantly changing trajectories of growth and vision.

Paul Trible, however, has been president of Christopher Newport since January 1996.

It's a long time for anyone, but particularly for Paul, whose longest prior service at a particular job was six years. Like many intense, successful, and visionary leaders, he tended to move on to new challenges. After law school, he clerked for a federal judge, worked as assistant U.S. Attorney, was elected at age 26 as one of Virginia's Commonwealth's Attorneys, and at 29 was elected to the U.S. House of Representatives for three terms, and then at 35 was elected to the United States Senate. Many in his party considered him an up-and-coming candidate for the presidency.

But even before his six-year Senate term ended, Paul decided not to run again. He had decided he wanted to invest his life in public service, yes, but in an arena where he could stimulate visionary change.

A few years later, he came to Christopher Newport.

When he did so, Paul Trible did indeed instigate extraordinary transformation early on. He sustained ongoing successes through some strong challenges. He and his administration, faculty, and staff created a new and better university than anyone could have dreamed. But, as noted, he did not move to fresh challenges after a few years. He stayed.

Why?

It's simple, says Paul, smiling. "I fell in love with this place."

CHAPTER 2

THEY OUGHT TO
BURN THIS PLACE

"We delight in the beauty of the butterfly, but rarely admit
the changes it has gone through to achieve that beauty."

— *MAYA ANGELOU*

W hen Paul Trible first walked the cracked cement sidewalks
of Christopher Newport in 1995, there was not a whole lot
to fall in love *with*. Founded in 1960 as a two-year preparatory branch
of the College of William & Mary, Christopher Newport College
gave an affordable higher education alternative to students from the
Tidewater area of Virginia. They could attend CNC for two years, then
finish their undergraduate degree at one of the state's many respected
institutions of higher learning. The school was led by an enterprising young director, later president, named Scotty Cunningham. He
had been on staff at William & Mary. He wrote, unforgettably, about
his trip to the abandoned building loaned by the city of Newport
News as the first home for the new college. It had been built in 1899.
There were ceilings at least 30 feet high, "rooms with wooden floors,
great state of disrepair, plaster hanging from the walls, lighting

fixtures askew. I walked into a classroom, and it had an old, pock-marked green blackboard...Scribbled across the board in yellow chalk was 'THEY OUGHT TO BURN THIS PLACE.'"[i]

With a great deal of grit and creativity, and funded by monies from the Virginia General Assembly, the head of the fledgling college hired faculty and staff, reviewed early applications, and Christopher Newport College opened for its 171 students in September 1961.

Scotty Cunningham stressed that he wanted the school to be a place marked by a commitment to quality, academic excellence, and relationships between students and faculty. Over the years the school grew, moved to a tract on its present location, and primarily served students in Newport News and the Peninsula area of Hampton Roads.

In 1969, CNC became a four-year college. Its second president arrived in 1970. In 1973, the General Assembly and State Commission on Higher Education hired an efficiency expert to review Virginia's state university system. Confidentially released to the legislators and commissioners, his report was unfortunately leaked to the local press. Among other conclusions, the author predicted that CNC would remain small, that its budget planning was poorly executed, its long-term planning was "completely inadequate," and that the institution should "be closed as quickly as conveniently possible."[ii]

Soon, however, the community rallied to support Christopher Newport. The Newport News Chamber of Commerce passed a resolution that emphasized the college's "great value to the 300,000 people...[of] the lower Peninsula."[iii] The powers that be rejected the closing of the college.

The spunky little school sailed on, though the episode "created a deep sense of inferiority and vulnerability among students and faculty," which marked the next decade of its development.[iv] Still, under the leadership of several more presidents over the years, CNC added a performing arts troupe and a 300-seat theater, which was used by campus and community alike. There were various clubs, a student newspaper, *The Captain's Log*, student government, basket-ball, tennis, golf, soccer, and other intercollegiate sports, as well as a plethora of intramural sports opportunities. There were cheerleaders to leap, yell, and wave pompoms as the school celebrated its newly bestowed "university" status in 1992. There was a mix of traditional and mostly part-time students, a four-year nursing program, some master's programs, a campus pub, and clubs.

There were great professors who cared about their students, and small classes. But it still felt like a commuter college, with little sense of campus life, spirit, or camaraderie. Many great accomplishments had been gained over the years, but the school was, in the words of its rector, still "unknown, under-appreciated, and underfunded."

After peaking with more than 5,000 students, enrollment started drifting downward. Other colleges nearby offered more classes on nights and weekends, which was more convenient for older students who had jobs and families. There were tensions between faculty and the administration. Administrators worried that the university would be swallowed up by another, larger, more proactive university. The newly constructed dormitory on campus was only half full of students...or half empty, depending on one's perspective. Less than nine percent of the students lived on campus. The angular buildings did not inspire visitors with their beauty. The landscaping budget, which had been perceived as an unnecessary line item, had been trimmed, though the few trees on campus had not. There was a parched feeling about the place, with haphazard cement walkways put in wherever students had happened to wear a path in the dry ground. Grass was scrubby, yellow, or nonexistent. Crabgrass, while plentiful, withered in the summer heat.

Today Christopher Newport University is routinely listed as one of the most beautiful college campuses in the United States. This is in no small part to those billion dollars invested in capital improvements to the undistinguished campus, which grew from 100 acres to 260 acres in size. Christopher Newport acquired 120 residential and commercial properties and completed more than 40 major construction projects. The grade point averages for incoming freshmen have risen from 2.8 in 1996 to 3.8 and are rising still in early 2022.

The operating budget went from $34 million a year to $172 million. The library grew from 330,000 volumes to more than 1.2 million. The endowment swelled from $300,000 to more than $60 million. The four-year graduation rate went from 11 percent to 69 percent, and the six-year rate from 35 percent to 80 percent. Student retention rates (from first-year to sophomore year) rose from 69 percent to 87 percent. The revamped, rigorous core curriculum received a perfect "A" by ACTA, the American Council of Trustees and Alumni, the only perfect score in any public institution in America.

Even with all this growth, class sizes got smaller, with the percentage of classes with 19 students or less moving from 44 percent in 1996 to 65 percent.

Such numbers give the overview of a transformed university. But how did it happen?

CHAPTER 3

THE SPACE BETWEEN THE SPEECHES

"Stories, narratives, and tales are our primary means for
both the creation and preservation of cultures, values,
and ambitions....without meaningful narratives that
abide and live and breathe, our organizations, societies
and governments grow sterile, lifeless and empty."

—*HENRY DOSS, FORBES*

T here are innumerable fine books on leadership, and many great
studies on trends in higher education. The goal here is not to
add to them for the adding's sake, but to document something as
unique as Christopher Newport itself. This is not a "business book,"
designed to distill marketplace principles to apply in commercial
enterprises. Nor is it a piece of investigative journalism that scru-
tinizes every controversy over the years. Nor is it an idealized tome
that denies rough spots ever existed, nor a cheery chronological list
of just when each new building on campus was completed or when
each distinguished faculty member arrived. Nor is it an overview of
the astounding amount of great academic courses, programs, clubs,
activities, student success services, charitable outreaches, and everything else that Christopher Newport offers.

This is a *story*. A story about what can happen when people of vision, creativity, and courage see potential in something that others may have written off. In that, the story of Christopher Newport University's transformation is interwoven with the stories of a cast of colorful characters, most notably, Paul and Rosemary Trible. But this is not a glowing biography or a memoir; Paul Trible has taken great pains to emphasize that this story is not about him. It's not a biography extolling his life events, nor a memoir sharing his innermost secrets. He is not that kind of guy.

That said, this tale *is* inevitably shaped and informed by Paul Trible's perspective. Others can write whatever they desire about Christopher Newport, but Paul Trible is the guy who, for more than two-and-a-half decades, developed a secret sauce that transformed this school. And in telling this story about the sauce, some transferrable truths about leadership, as well as service, community, and significance inexorably emerge. So perhaps this small book might pass them on.

As both anthropologists and management gurus will tell you, "tribal stories" are crucial for any community or organizational entity. Our early ancestors passed on powerful oral traditions that transferred the shaping stories of the tribe to the next generation, and the next. Every family has such stories, tales of great-great-grandmother Harriet or Pearl or whomever, and how the generations of old dreamed big dreams, sweated, and sacrificed to make a place in the world for those who would follow them.

The stories take on a life of their own, and from these narratives of beginnings, the tribe, or the family members, have a sense of identity. The same is true in 21st century corporations, no matter how virtual, or in institutions of higher learning, or cultures at large. Where did we come from? Who are we, really? And what do we stand for? If a community loses its thread of common answers to such questions, its members lose their distinctive tapestry of the past, their shared vision for the future, and their actual connectivity in the present.

Connectivity is a technical word. It evokes platforms, systems, and applications. When our phones or laptops don't have it, we can't communicate or share resources. We are isolated. The same is true in our relationships within a system, or group of human beings, except in that context we rarely talk about "connectivity." That would be weird. No, we use a different word. What creates connection in a community of human beings, even if they are quite different from one another, is a shared sense of origins, respect, empathy, and affection. You might even call it love.

Now, *there's* a word you don't hear often in leadership books or higher education treatises. But if there was ever a key word for the secret sauce at Christopher Newport, that's it.

In playwright George Bernard Shaw's words, made more famous when his quote was paraphrased by Senator Robert Kennedy during his 1968 campaign for the presidential nomination, "Some men see things as they are, and say 'why?' I dream of things that never were, and say 'why not?'" Decades ago, when others saw Christopher Newport as modest and second-class, Paul Trible saw a gleaming, competitive, premier public university. He didn't see what CNU was; he saw what it could be.

Or to put it more accurately, Paul *did* see what the school was, and he loved it anyway. That love is what made him care enough, and what gave him enough passionate impetus, to initiate transformational change.

Paul and his indispensable, long-time executive assistant, Beverley Mueller, recently dug up his handwritten notes from his very first speech after he was named president of Christopher Newport. Written in Paul's firm backhand on a yellow legal pad, the ideas flowed smoothly, quickly, decisively, as if Paul was receiving some sort of inner dictation. There are few cross outs. And after languishing for 25 years in a file cabinet, those jottings sound as if Paul could have written them yesterday.

Those notes shaped Paul's remarks to the Christopher Newport Board of Visitors when the Board voted to appoint Paul as the university's new president back in 1995. Some of it might sound like the type of soaring rhetoric any new president or CEO might utter on his first day. But those notes show far more: this guy knew exactly where he was going, strategically...and he did it.

"CNU is in the business of transforming people's lives, and making our community and our commonwealth a better place to live and work...Christopher Newport is a very special place. Here we put students first. We have a caring community where the emphasis is on superb teaching in small classrooms.

"We celebrate our diversity. Our students of all ages are interested in making a difference in this world. We are the face of the 21st century and our success will ensure the success of our community and our commonwealth."

Paul went on to acknowledge the fact that he was not a life-long member of the academy. He had a long-term love for the liberal arts and sciences, and during his teaching stint at Harvard he had learned something about inspiring students.

He talked about communicating with "passion and persuasion the vision and good work of Christopher Newport." He talked about *how* he would equip the university to make transformational change for the better.

"We will immediately engage new friends in Richmond and Washington. We will work together to increase the enrollment and retention of good students. And we will dramatically increase the financial resources available to the university to expand and enhance our facilities, to better pay our faculty and staff, to provide more financial assistance to our students and to always improve the quality of the education we offer."

Paul acknowledged the great gifts of those who had preceded him at Christopher Newport and went on to declare "a new era" to the university. "Our job is to unleash the energy, enthusiasm, commitment, and rich talents that abound in this university, and we will do it together...My door will always be open to each of you. If you have a good idea, a problem, complaint, or simply want to let off some steam—come and see me. I will be walking around this campus. Listening, asking questions, being available.

"And you know, it's time to think and act like winners. We will not tolerate those who say, 'it can't be done,' or 'it can only be done this way.' We will not allow others to limit our dreams or diminish our success."

Paul talked about the strategic plan that he would develop, with collaboration, in the next 60 days. He talked about raising money, building new buildings, and increasing enrollment.

"But our primary purpose—yours and mine—is to establish CNU as a university of choice for all Virginians. To ensure to all those who walk this beautiful campus—students, faculty, staff—a richly rewarding educational experience...

"Together we will settle for nothing less than our <u>best.</u>

Together we will settle for nothing less than <u>success.</u>

So, strap on your seatbelts: this university is getting ready to soar."

Paul Trible's soaring strategic intentions in that first official speech at Christopher Newport in late 1995 sprang out of an essential vision that has not changed since. All the plans, all the changes, all the remarkable transformations that you'll read about in this story, these grew from the conviction that Christopher Newport exists to equip students to lead lives of *significance*. Academic, career, and financial successes are to be celebrated, of course. But human beings are meant to seek more than a life of material success. So, Christopher Newport seeks not just to instruct minds but to inspire hearts, equipping young people to become intentional adults who lead lives of meaning, consequence, service, and purpose, seeking to make the world a better place.

Paul says, "Everything we've done over the past few decades—including our rigorous core curriculum of the liberal arts and sciences, our nationally respected leadership program, our honor code, our focus on community service, our soaring architecture and magnificent campus, our culture of respect—has been to make this 'life of significance' a reality."

We've all been to funerals where we've heard life referred to as the "dash between the dates." Every gravestone has a date of birth and a date of death with a dash between the two, and life is lived in that space.

We can adjust the metaphor for the framing structure for this book. It's about the "space between the speeches." This space would be the decades between Paul Trible's first speech at Christopher Newport and whenever that last speech occurs. At this writing that final address has not yet happened, though Paul has set his retirement for 2022. But the story of this book is about those many years between Paul's beginnings at CNU and his retirement. It's about the incredible changes and growth that he brought to the university, and the extraordinary team—students, faculty, administrators, staff, parents, neighbors, community leaders, and other like-minded people—who pulled together to make an impossible dream come true.

That story, of course, won't end with Paul Trible's retirement or the comings or goings of any other leader. It's a story that will carry forward, lived by ongoing generations of young people who come to Christopher Newport and are awakened to a robust vision of a life of significance. Not just academic achievement and eventual business and professional success, but the deeper sort of purpose-driven life of significance that finds its nexus in loving one's neighbor as oneself and doing good for one's fellow human beings wherever and however one can.

CHAPTER 4

WHO IS PAUL TRIBLE
AND WHERE DID HE
COME FROM?

"Life is no 'brief candle' to me. It is a sort of splendid torch which I have got hold of for a moment,
and I want to make it burn as brightly as possible
before handing it on to the future generations."

— *GEORGE BERNARD SHAW*

A s we've noted, Paul Trible has been adamant that this book should
not focus on him, but on the story of Christopher Newport
University. His humility is admirable, but we cannot allow it to skew
the narrative arc of this story. Any community is a tapestry of its
various members, and the quirks, eccentricities, and unique backgrounds of each individual make up a whole that is more than the
sum of its parts. And the leader's personal narrative reveals important insights on the character that shaped this university in its most
formative decades.

Paul Trible was not born in a log cabin. He didn't walk six miles
through the snow to school every day, like everyone's great-great-grand-
father, nor did he split logs for a living and study by the light of the

fire at night, like an Abraham Lincoln. But his childhood does evoke a slower time that no longer seems to exist.

Paul's father, Paul Trible, Sr., was the seventh child of a seventh son, born and raised in Virginia's Essex County on a family farm that a branch of the Trible family still owns. Paul's dad went to Virginia Tech and graduated with honors with a degree in business administration in 1933. In 1942 he married Katherine Schlipp. He served in the Pacific during World War II, and then returned home to his career at the International Salt Company, from which he would eventually retire as vice president of marketing.

Paul Trible was born in 1946. He would be an only child. His mother was a homemaker, and as a boy Paul knew that "she loved me more than anything else in the world." His dad was a tall man who, unlike many men of his generation, had no problem expressing affection for his son in public. Paul grew up with a strong sense of love, confidence, and potential. "I was instructed and inspired by the way my mom and dad lived their lives," he would say many years after their deaths. "It was not a formal instruction process. I loved them. I embraced their values. I wanted to make them proud and live a life that made a difference."

Mill Creek flowed past Gascony, the family property, with the Great Wicomico River and the Chesapeake Bay just beyond. When Paul was about 10, he had a little boat, a five-and-a-half horsepower Johnson. He was just strong enough to pull the starter cord and get it going. Perhaps channeling sea captain Christopher Newport without even knowing it, he loved being out on the water, independent, seeking new adventures...though he was instructed to always stay within sight of his mother.

Paul would tie his boat to an oyster stake and sit for hours, fishing. The occasional eagle would soar overhead. The leaves of the huge trees on shore would shimmer in the breeze. He caught dozens of tiny fish that looked big to him; he'd bring them back to his mom, who would clean them and fry them up for supper. Once a week Paul would cross the creek to a neighboring property owned by his cousin, Billy Blackwell. Billy had cows, and he would give Paul an enormous jug filled with milk, heavy cream floating on the top. Paul would secure it in his boat and bring it home. Paul would also live in Richmond, New Orleans, and Pennsylvania, but Gascony was always home.

When it came time for college, Paul was accepted at the University of Virginia, but he wanted the experience of a smaller school. He figured that if he went to law school later, he could do so at a larger university. He went to Virginia's Hampden-Sydney College, founded in 1775, the tenth oldest institution of higher learning in the U.S. It was, and is, one of the few remaining private colleges that specializes in educating and developing young men. Its mission—"to form good men and good citizens in an atmosphere of sound learning"—strikes a chord of recognition with anyone who knows Paul Trible.

His academic advisor was the chair of the English department, one Dr. Hassell Algernon Simpson. Paul sat in a chair across from the professor's cluttered desk. Thousands of books spilled from bookshelves on every wall of the office.

"What do you want to do with your life?" asked Dr. Hassell Algernon Simpson. "You have to begin with the end in mind, you know."

Paul felt a little unnerved, but he spoke right up.

"I want to be president of the United States."

Dr. Simpson nodded and reached for his pipe. This young man seemed to know where he wanted to go.

"I'm not sure exactly where that came from," the seventy-something Paul Trible says today. "But public service used to be a noble thing. In my growing-up years, I was always mindful of the huge contributions that Virginians had made in the founding of this republic. Virginia was the birthplace of George Washington. James Madison. James Monroe. My parents were never political, but they imparted to me this notion that I should lead a meaningful life. Wanting to be president seemed a worthy aspiration, particularly since I'd been raised in Virginia in the shadow of these leaders who had contributed so immeasurably to the creation of this country."

How does an 18-year-old kid learn to think in these terms?

Bobby Hatten is one of Paul Trible's oldest friends. Bobby is an energetic, enormously successful trial lawyer with an impressive thatch of thick white hair that used to be red back when he and Paul were 18 and 19-year-olds at Hampden-Sydney. He says that Paul was "quiet, serious-minded, well liked, smart, and studious" back then. He wasn't in student government and didn't play sports. Bobby would become more politically progressive over the years, but back in the day he and Paul were in the Republican club together. They both majored in history.

Paul says his years at Hampden-Sydney strengthened his notions of honor, service, and contribution to civic society. There were also a few water balloon incidents and some unremarkable fraternity parties. He went on to law school at Washington and Lee, joined a year later by his buddy Bobby Hatten.

"In law school Paul became much more engaged," Bobby says. "He quickly made the *Law Review*, and after he graduated, he became a law clerk to Judge Bryan in federal court in Alexandria, Virginia."

Bobby says that this is what really changed Paul's life. He was clerking in federal court, getting to see the "big leagues, the best lawyers" in action. "Every day he had to write opinions, or orders, subjected to editing from Judge Bryan. Stuff would get torn apart if it wasn't just right." Bobby says that this experience, and Paul's later work as a federal prosecutor, sharpened Paul's clarity of argument, articulation, persuasiveness, and his power as a communicator.

Paul served as assistant U.S. attorney in Alexandria, then pursued his political career as Commonwealth's Attorney.

It was during his first week of law school that Paul received what he calls the single most important gift in his life: he met Rosemary Dunaway, an effervescent and outgoing young woman at Sweet Briar College, on a blind date. Rosemary had been chosen America's Junior Miss—a scholarship program for distinguished young women—in 1967. Paul and Rosemary continued dating after she transferred to the University of Texas. They were married in the fall of 1971, after he had finished law school and she'd completed her undergraduate degree.

Bobby Hatten says, "By now Paul had a magnetic ease of speaking with people. He was genuinely interested in them, and Rosemary was the gorgeous, friendly girl next door who could talk to the governor or a soda pop salesperson with equal ease and interest. The two of them were symbiotic; together they were synergistic."

Back in 1974, when Paul Trible was Commonwealth's Attorney (an elected position), he prosecuted a colorful case that involved three prison escapees who had allegedly stolen a car, robbed a bank in Essex County at gunpoint, and gotten into a shootout with the state police when they were pursued, after which they were apprehended.

As Paul made his case in the historic old Essex County Courthouse, an elderly, dignified African American man watched him from the gallery. One day during the lunch recess, he approached Paul, who was 27 at the time.

"Mr. Trible," he said. "My name is William Willis. I knew your grandfather, and he was a good man. I'm going to help you in your next election."

He had Paul's attention. William Willis grew up in Essex County, and like many young Black citizens of the south in the early 1900s, he moved north to find a job. He lived in Philadelphia, where he eventually got involved in precinct politics and learned useful political lessons. He worked hard to get people who were inactive to register to vote. He set up rides for people to get to the polls. And when he returned to Virginia, he continued his political activism.

As a young man, William had known Paul's grandfather, George Meredith Trible. And back then, when the South was segregated, George Trible had treated William and his family with genuine respect and kindness. William had never forgotten it.

So now, he had found George Trible's grandson. Paul never even knew his grandfather, who had died before Paul was born.

Mr. Willis' savvy political support would help Paul enormously in his first run for Congress in 1976. He spoke up for Paul in all his communities of influence. He helped pro-Trible voters get to the polls. He invited Paul and Rosemary to visit and speak at his church. Paul, a self-described uptight Episcopalian, was not comfortable with the notion of speaking from the pulpit.

"Oh," drawled Mr. Willis, a life-long Baptist, "if we could get more politicians in church, we'd have a lot less trouble in this world." Under

Mr. Willis' tutelage, Paul got comfortable worshipping and speaking in religious communities of color. He visited homes, listened to his hosts' life stories, and sipped lemonade on every front porch in the county.

And in the end, Paul won the election, and pulled in nearly 80 percent of the votes in Essex County.

"My grandfather gave kindness and respect to a young William Willis," Paul says, "and decades and decades later, Mr. Willis returned that gift to a grandson my grandfather never even knew. It taught me that the good we do to others makes a difference not only in that moment, but also makes an impact we will likely never see, far beyond."

Several years later, Paul ran for Congress. Before the election, his old friend Bobby Hatten planned a Newport News fundraiser for Paul's campaign. Bobby invited all his friends and business contacts on the Peninsula, and arranged for great quantities of shrimp, beer, and wine to be set out for a casual yet festive gathering. It turned out to be somewhat less than successful.

"I am positive that we did not have more than 10 people attend," Bobby says today. No matter. After that Paul developed great relationships with influential businesspeople in Newport News; they—and their friends—pulled for Trible for Congress.

When all this was going on in 1976, Virginia had been a blue state since Reconstruction. Paul was running as a Republican in this year that Democrat Jimmy Carter would sweep the South for the Presidency. Meanwhile, in Virginia's First District race, Paul was a 28-year-old prosecutor from a rural community with no ties to the populist Peninsula of Virginia, where his opponent served as a senior legislator.

Paul, Rosemary, and their team of volunteers spent the steamy summer prior to the election knocking on doors all over the district. (The most enthusiastic volunteer, Rosemary, was pregnant at the time; she passed out on someone's front porch in York County, so, over her protests, she was taken off the door-to-door team.)

Paul started going to Newport News Shipbuilding's front gates every morning at 6 a.m. He needed the blue-collar vote, which typically went Democratic. He would say hello, shake hands, and try to connect with the workers. At first, he was met with absolute indifference. He kept at it. Eventually workers started nodding or even saying hello; sometimes they'd stop for a second. Some would actually give Paul an encouraging word in his congressional race, and a growing number told him they'd vote for him. Maybe they felt sorry for him. Everyone knew he was the underdog.

Election night came. Paul, Rosemary, and the rest of their team were at the Ramada Inn in Newport News, listening to the news as returns slowly came in. The other candidate was strong in urban areas; Paul's strength would be in the rural districts whose results were last to be tallied.

As it got later, Paul was still behind, but was gaining on his opponent.

"It's better to be a congressman for a few hours than never at all," Paul told his team cheerfully. "Let's go claim victory!"

They trooped down to the hotel ballroom, jammed with hundreds of supporters, red, white, and blue, balloons, and other election accoutrements. The ballroom resounded with cheers as Paul thanked everyone for their help in achieving this great win. Then everyone went off to bed.

Miraculously, early in the morning, Paul discovered he really *had* won. A national news commentator announced that a "nobody from nowhere" had just won Virginia's First District congressional race. The nobody and Rosemary went down to Newport News Shipbuilding and stood at the front gates, greeting the workers as they streamed in for their morning shift. Paul had carried Newport News City with 50.5 percent of the vote to his opponent's 46.6 percent. (A third candidate got the rest.)

"Thank you!" they called out to people. "We are so grateful for your help! Thanks for your support!"

"What happened then was one of the most magical moments of my life," Paul said later. "Within moments everyone knew that I had come back to thank everyone." People gathered around him, slapping him on the back, shaking his hand, giving him high fives. "For years after that, people would come up to me and say, 'I was at the shipyard gates that morning when you came back to say thank you. That's how we knew you were real. No one ever does that!'"

In the following two elections, Paul won that congressional district with more than 70 percent and then more than 90 percent of the vote. His friends in the shipyard did not let him down.

Paul served three terms in Congress, then ran for the United States Senate. He won. He was 35 years old. It was now 1982. Ronald Reagan—the "sunny president"—was in the Oval Office. Paul was a rising star in the Republican Party, part of an elite pool of 100 U.S. senators, and a good deal closer to his long-held aspiration to be president of the United States.

As we've said, however, before his first six-year term was up, Paul decided not to run again. He had seen the glacial pace of the Senate and how difficult it was to create big-scale, transformational changes. He had seen the enormous toll that government service at this level took on his colleagues. Too few had strong relationships with their spouses and families. The time pressures were enormous. Paul decided that the benefits were too slim, the costs too high. He wanted to invest time with his young son and daughter; he wanted to work in partnership with his wife rather than constantly be apart from her. He wanted to use the gifts he'd been given in a place where he could truly benefit a community in an enduring way.

Paul's lifelong aspiration would come true. He did indeed become president. But not of the United States. He became president of Christopher Newport University. He had begun with the right end in mind, he just had the wrong context. Or, as he would put it, he'd climbed near the top of the ladder, to find out that he had his ladder against the wrong wall.

CHAPTER 5

CONVERGENCE

"I can do things you cannot, you can do things
I cannot; together we can do great things."
—*MOTHER TERESA*

P aul Trible left the Senate in 1989. He spent time with his wife,
went to his kids' plays and sports events, and laughed with
his family at the dinner table. He was a teaching fellow at Harvard
University's Kennedy School of Government for a semester, then
practiced law with a D.C. firm and led The Jefferson Group, a government relations and business consulting firm. He was convinced by his
party to run for the Republican nomination for governor of Virginia
but lost in the primary. He was content.

Paul Trible knew of Christopher Newport because the school was
in the congressional district he had represented, and he had given a
commencement address there. In 1994, when his old friend George
Allen had become governor of the Commonwealth, he had let Paul
know that he would like to appoint him to the Board of Visitors for
one of Virginia's 15 four-year colleges and universities. These are the
schools' governing bodies, their members appointed by the governor
for four-year terms.

George Allen asked Paul where he would like to serve. Paul thought about it. Virginia's great schools like the University of Virginia and William & Mary had thrived with excellence for hundreds of years... but how does one really contribute to an institution like that? At best you would be operating in the margins.

Christopher Newport was Virginia's youngest university. It was struggling to survive. It presented many opportunities for demonstrable change. "Maybe I could really make a difference there," Paul told George Allen. He asked to be appointed to CNU's board.

The governor complied.

Paul walked the pitted sidewalks of the school. He talked to students, who were usually in a hurry to get to class or, after class, to leave campus and get to their jobs. He longed to do something to tap into the potential he sensed in this place. He thought about when he and Rosemary had first campaigned for the House of Representatives, back when he was 28 years old. Christopher Newport was right in the middle of Virginia's 1st congressional district. The people in the community had gradually warmed to the young Paul Trible. They had supported him in his crucial first election, and his second, and third. He wanted to do something to pay back the community, to help as he had once been helped.

Soon after this, in 1995, Christopher Newport commenced a search for a new president. President Tony Santoro had been at the university since 1987 and had shepherded the school through its transition from Christopher Newport College to University in 1992. He had spearheaded the building of the first residence hall on campus, which bore his name. He had presided over the old Ferguson High School's incorporation into CNU's campus in the mid-1990s, which would lay the groundwork for further expansion. But the Board of Visitors decided that it was a season for new leadership at Christopher Newport, and Dr. Santoro agreed it was time for a change. The Board created a presidential search committee, which consisted of a cross-section of university and community leaders, including Paul Trible.

Cindi Perry had been on staff at Christopher Newport for 17 years, having come there right after she graduated from William & Mary. She had directed Christopher Newport's planning and budget, and knew the school inside and out. She served on the search committee, as did a financial executive and former CNU rector named Alan Witt.

Alan had first come to Christopher Newport as a 16-year-old, first-year student in 1972. He was a smart and precocious kid whose dad had just moved the family to Newport News. He majored in accounting, and in the spring of 1976 met Paul Trible at a political event, when Alan was president of CNU's Young Republicans. (There were two in the club.)

After Alan's graduation that May, he worked with an accounting firm called Eggleston Smith before starting his own firm with three associates in 1979, at the tender age of 24. The firm, eventually named PBMares, became one of the top 100 accounting and business consulting companies of the 44,000 accounting firms in America.

Alan also worked in state politics, along with both Republican and Democratic governors of the Commonwealth. He served on local boards of directors, got involved in all kinds of public service opportunities, and in 1985 Governor Chuck Robb appointed Alan to his alma mater's Board of Visitors.

As Alan remembers the early actions of the search committee, "We ran an ad in the *Chronicle of Higher Education* and went through other avenues. Each applicant was more underwhelming than the prior. CNU just was not attractive to the talent we were looking for."

The committee had also commissioned an outside consultant to develop a recommendation for the type of president who could best serve the ailing school. On the evening that the consultant presented her findings, the committee met in a small, windowless room in Christopher Newport's old student union. There was a long wooden conference table that filled most of the space. The consultant sat at one end, and the committee members crowded around the sides. The expert gave her report, which unsurprisingly concluded that the university needed strong leadership and a clear vision for its future.

She also recommended that the search committee look not just in the academy, but to people of experience in business, government, and beyond the academic world.

These recommendations confirmed something inside of Paul. He looked at the people gathered around the conference table and cleared his throat. "I don't have a PhD," he said. "I haven't labored in the academic world. But I have learned important lessons in government service. I know and love this community and Virginia, and I've come to know and love this school. I think I want to apply for the presidency of Christopher Newport, and I want you to tell me if this is something I should do."

There was silence.

"Do you have any questions for me?" Paul asked.

Crickets.

"Well," he concluded. "Why don't I leave, and you all discuss this, and if you think that this isn't a good idea, then we won't pursue it further." The committee had 84 resumes to review, and he wanted to make sure the group members were unanimous in whatever they decided; perhaps, in their estimation, he was not the person for the job.

Paul went home to his wife and family. The rest of the committee members stared at each other in "stunned silence," as they later told the media. "All of us just had no words," Cindi Perry said. "This was not a development we could have dreamed of."

There were two faculty members on the committee, neither of them "shrinking violets," according to Cindi. Both were the absolute opposite of Paul, politically speaking; but both faculty members bought in almost instantly. "It just felt right to everyone," Cindi says today. "The question was, how do we do this, logistically?"

Alan Witt was on a business trip to Atlanta and had not been able to attend the surprising meeting. This was in the pre-cell phone era, and he started getting reams of telephone messages that night at his hotel. They were from other members of the search committee. He called Cindi Perry. She told him about the consultant's report and Paul Trible's unexpected response.

"Senator Trible dropped this bombshell on us and left the room for us to decide," she told Alan. "There are three of us who are employees; we can't talk about this with anyone else on campus. We've spent hours discussing this...We really need your input."

"Give me 30 minutes," said Alan.

He sat at the desk in his hotel room, and in good accountant style, made a T chart about the notion of Trible as president, with negatives on one side and positives on the other. He sat back and reflected on it. There was no question in his mind as to what would be best for Christopher Newport.

He called Cindi back. "This is an opportunity too good for us to pass up," he said.

Paul, of course, was not particularly aware of the constant buzz and hours of confidential discussion his announcement had created. He was consulting with the person who mattered the most. His wife.

"Paul has always been someone who's able to have a vision of what's around the corner," Rosemary Trible says today. "Sometimes it has shocked me. The idea of his becoming president of CNU was just not something I saw coming."

Rosemary wondered what this dramatic change might mean for their family and home life. Their daughter was getting ready to leave for college; their son was 16. The Tribles had just built a beautiful home in Williamsburg; it was to be the place where they would settle, raise their children, and peacefully live out the rest of their post-political private lives. An antiques connoisseur with a keen eye for décor and design, Rosemary was just putting the finishing touches on their new home. It was to be featured in Virginia's annual Garden Tour the following spring. The notion of moving to Newport News and living in the CNU-owned president's house, at the time an old, aesthetically challenged rancher, was a little hard for her to digest.

But Rosemary had seen her husband's love for Christopher Newport. She knew he had a sense of calling to make a difference at CNU. She drove to Christopher Newport's campus. She parked and watched the students walk between the plain buildings. A person with strong emotional antennae, she just didn't sense any spark, any sense of enthusiasm from anyone. There was no "campus feeling."

A person of faith, Rosemary sat in her car and prayed. Resolutely. "God," she said. "If this is where you want us, I'm willing. Can we make a difference here?" She sat for a while. A sense of quiet came over her spirit.

The answer, as far as she could discern, was yes. Yes.

Rosemary headed home to Williamsburg. "Okay," she said to her enterprising husband. "If the powers that be approve this, let's go forward."

A week later the chair of the search committee, also Christopher Newport's rector, called Paul. His name was David Peebles; he was the CEO of Ferguson Enterprises, based in Newport News, which would later become the United States' largest distributor of plumbing supplies. David didn't see any need to mess around when a great decision was obvious.

"Paul," he said. "The search committee has met three times in the past week without you, and we are unanimous that you should be CNU's new president. So we've disbanded the search committee and are prepared to recommend your selection to the Board of Visitors."

The announcement that the Board of Visitors had unanimously approved former congressperson and U. S. Senator Paul Trible as the fifth president of Christopher Newport University took the media, and just about everybody else, by surprise.

To some, it seemed too good to be true. Others were concerned about Paul's lack of long-term experience in academia.

One such skeptic was a conservative political analyst and radio talk show host named Bill Thomas. Bill believed that a college education prepares and equips citizens, regardless of their color or community of origin, so they can contribute to the quality of life in America. Governor Allen appointed him to begin a term on Christopher Newport's Board of Visitors in mid-1996. He knew that Paul Trible was well respected in the Black community. But he didn't know if Paul had what it would take to rescue CNU. Never one to be shy about judiciously speaking his mind, today he says that at the time when Paul took the helm, Christopher Newport was a sinking educational institution. Bill respected Paul's political experience, but, as he told members of the media, "I was just concerned about not having an expert running the university. If I needed someone to build a ship for me, I would get a ship builder."[v]

(As we'll see, Bill Thomas listened to what Paul said, watched what he did, and went on to become one of Paul's most stalwart allies.)

And back in 1996, some critics felt like Paul's compensation package was a stretch. The Board of Visitors approved an annual salary that was significantly higher than the previous president's. "When you're looking for a miracle worker, you've got to pay a miracle worker," explained Rector Peebles.

On Paul and Rosemary's part, however, it was a hundred thousand dollars a year pay cut. But no matter. This was not just a job for them. It was a calling.

Paul commenced his term as Christopher Newport's fifth president on January 2, 1996.

CHAPTER 6

CRAZY AS HELL

"Courage is the most important of all the
virtues because without courage, you can't
practice any other virtue consistently."

— *MAYA ANGELOU*

S ome of the first things Paul Trible did at Christopher Newport
when he arrived in 1996 were pretty low-tech, but high in
symbolism and impact. Paul walked the campus quite a bit, talking
with students, meeting with their interest groups, and attending
athletic events. He taught an evening course titled 'Leadership in
Politics.' He met with faculty and administrators. He listened.

During his first week as president, Paul considered the parking lot.
All the closest spots lined up near the administration building had
stern signs claiming them for the president, vice presidents, deans,
and other administrators.

Paul called all these important people together.

"When you go to MacDonald's," he asked, "are all the parking places
near the front door reserved for the people who work there, or for
the customers?"

His colleagues smiled. "The customers."

"Well," continued Paul, "who are our customers?"

Lightbulbs. "The *students*."

A day or two later, with a photographer in tow, Paul went out to the parking lot and pulled down the "reserved" sign marked "President" and put up a sign marked "Students." Within minutes, it seemed, the news had made its way around campus even before the photo appeared in the school newspaper. It was a small thing, but Paul had underscored his point more powerfully than he could have in any speech: *at Christopher Newport, students come first.*

Then there was the aesthetic issue of the crabby grass and the nonexistent landscaping. Paul had sworn to himself that he would get that campus looking green and beautiful if he had to spray paint the lawns. He knew that first impressions were key, and if the campus looked uncared for, why would any prospective student even want to take a second look at Christopher Newport?

He revived the fading landscaping budget. He called a friend, a retired army officer named Bob Goodhart who had a great love for trees, plants, and shrubs. After his retirement Bob had created a landscaping business. Paul invited Bob over to the campus.

"Listen," he said. "You can change the world one lawn at a time, or you can come here and create a masterpiece."

It was an appealing challenge. Bob left his business and came to Christopher Newport, where he built up a team to keep things green, lush, and lovely. And yes, early on he conspired with Paul to paint the grass green a time or two before particularly important campus events. His team installed irrigation systems and planted trees and shrubbery adjacent to some of the existing buildings to hide their harsh lines. He built sidewalks of classic interlocking brick pavers.

It was obvious that this wasn't the old Christopher Newport anymore.

Paul also put his political skills into play. During his political service on Capitol Hill, the atmosphere was rather different from what it has become in recent years. There was more talk, less shouting. More civility. Governance had to take place in the middle, and lawmakers of different points of view could actually hammer out compromises. Paul was a conservative in terms of his views of the nature of government, but he worked well with, and developed relationships with, members of Congress who held more liberal philosophies. He had never been a reactionary or a bomb thrower and enjoyed a good reputation as a reasonable negotiator. So, by the time he got to Christopher Newport he was well positioned to work with Virginia's General Assembly, which of course held the purse strings for all of the Commonwealth's public institutions of higher learning.

At the time, the key relationship in the General Assembly was with a power broker par excellence named Alan Diamonstein. An attorney and long-term representative in the Virginia House of Delegates, he served as chair of the education appropriations subcommittee. Progressive in his political views, he and Paul could have been adversaries, but they had become friends during Paul's time in the House of Representatives and the Senate. Paul had helped the Tidewater community, and now Alan looked favorably as Paul shared his brimming enthusiasm for the great things that were going to happen at Christopher Newport.

But things didn't look good for the upcoming budget negotiations in Richmond. Governor Allen's previously released budget proposal had included a sad 4.9 percent increase for Christopher Newport. Paul met with political influencers all over the state, sharing his vision and the need for funding to improve the university as something Virginia could be proud of. When that first round of budget negotiations ended, not even three months into Paul Trible's presidency, the General Assembly gave CNU a 21.4 percent increase in funding—the largest increase of any university in the state. The new money went in part toward long-delayed faculty raises, renovations of existing buildings, and improvements in computer resources. Monies were also approved toward the planning of a sports and convocation center and a second residential hall. There was also a little nugget of $5 million for a performing arts center, which we will come to in a moment.

The happy attentions of the General Assembly helped ease some of the skepticism, but there were cynical murmurs as faculty, staff, and administration listened to a key speech Paul gave at the university 90 days after he arrived at Christopher Newport in the beginning of 1996.

The speech would brim with the phrases and the vision that he would articulate over and over the decades to come. "You have to repeat the vision so people will hear it and embrace it themselves," Rosemary says about her husband's intentional communication style. "And people are always watching. Everything you do and say must reinforce the values and the vision. They need to hear it over and over again, so it is recorded in their minds and memory."

So even as Paul Trible laid out specific plans for the school, he also painted the big picture of the great opportunities ahead for Christopher Newport.

"We reject the notion of incremental progress. We are in the business of dramatic transformation, and everything we do will be done at the highest level of excellence.

"Most universities are in the business of training minds. We care about both minds and hearts. Our job is to enrich minds and stir hearts. We will equip and challenge our students to lead lives of leadership, honor, and service. We will create a tradition of service to those less fortunate, of servant leadership, of caring for others in our university community. This is a place where students will learn how to live, not just how to earn a living.

"First impressions matter. We will create one of the most beautiful campuses in America. Nothing instructs and inspires more than great art and architecture. We will build great buildings of civic proportions and classical beauty. And we will create, right here, one of America's preeminent public liberal arts and sciences universities. We will establish CNU as a university of choice for every Virginian. We will challenge our students to choose to lead lives of significance... to lead and love and engage and set the world on fire!"

This last line, a Paul Trible classic, originated with St. Catherine of Siena, a 14th century Dominican nun. Known for her service to the poor and her involvement in politics, St. Catherine wrote, "Be who God meant you to be and you will set the world on fire."

Paul quickly found the people in the administration who had a similar sense of spirit to his own. He asked Cindi Perry to become his chief of staff, a job title that at the time sounded a lot more like Capitol Hill than it did the halls of academia. She would work with Paul for 25 years, one of his chief "co-conspirators," as Paul called Rosemary as well as his other closest allies in the great adventure of transforming Christopher Newport.

Cindi says that "if you read one of Paul's speeches, it may not seem particularly powerful. But he is an amazing speaker. He has a way, in person, of painting word pictures, that, even in tough times, make you believe that the impossible can be achieved. His enthusiasm and passion are contagious. He would talk about CNU, and everyone would start getting excited. That just hadn't happened before."

Paul's larger theme was the ongoing pursuit of excellence. Cindi says, "We were a beleaguered college community that had slowly drifted into and accepted mediocrity. In his first days as president, Paul made it well known that we would no longer accept anything less than striving for excellence—whether it involved academics, athletics, buildings, grounds, or whatever. It was never a choice between bigger or better, the answer was always "better." If it couldn't be done well, it wasn't done."

Quentin Kidd, a trim, bearded political scientist who is now Dean of Christopher Newport's College of Social Sciences and Director of the Wason Center for Civic Leadership, arrived at CNU as a professor of political science in 1997.

After graduating from high school, Quentin had served in the Army as part of Operation Desert Storm. His combat experiences in Iraq had caused him to reflect on all kinds of existential questions. *Why am I here? How did I come out okay and others did not?* Encouraged by his sergeant, he had gone on to college, then to graduate school. His political science studies provoked his interest in southern politics; the South, as a region, has gone through more major and convulsive change than other parts of the country, and its politics raise important questions, both regional and national, about civic engagement and the role of citizens in creating a just society.

Quentin's graduate work had been at large universities. When he arrived at Christopher Newport in the fall of 1997, he thought he would teach political science for a year or two and then move on. CNU was just too small for him. The first course Quentin taught was a night class made up of 17 women, all older than him, and one 18-year-old who did not return after the first week. The kid evidently did not want to be in a class full of moms.

Each week there was a break in the three-hour class. Quentin, an ultra-marathoner, was hungry all the time. During the break, he'd pull open his backpack, scrounge around, and devour three or four energy bars before it was time to resume his lecture.

By the third week of class, when the mid-class break arrived, the women all reached into their own big bags and brought out a bunch of covered dishes, paper plates, and plastic silverware. Macaroni and cheese. Deviled eggs. Chicken salad. Comfort food.

Everyone would break bread together, talk, and then get back Zto class. "It was the first time I really got to know students," Quentin says today. "There had been more than 400 students in the last class I'd taught at my former university. I'd stand in front of a microphone, teach, and leave. Now I was getting to know people; I'm still in touch with some of them today, decades later."

Quentin got hooked, if not on macaroni and cheese, at least on the faculty-student relationships that a smaller school can make possible. He started holding office hours at the school's campus cafe. One day Paul Trible walked by. "He" sat down to talk; the two shared a cup of coffee and got to know one another a bit. "I liked what he was envisioning," Quentin says.

As a younger—and then untenured—member of the faculty, Quentin was more positive about change than some of his more gray and staid colleagues. Still, he felt that Paul underestimated the kinds of reactions his ideas would receive.

"Academics are trained to be skeptical," Quentin explains. "And Paul had also gotten some resistance rooted in the community. Traditionally speaking, particularly in the years before the Jefferson Lab and other higher tech companies had come to the area, Newport News had a blue-collar identity. The shipyard employed 40,000 people. There was a sense of skepticism that change can really happen. Life is constrained; your possibilities for moving up are limited. It made it hard for many in the community to envision the kind of changes Paul was talking about."

As Quentin remembers it, when Paul became president of Christopher Newport, Paul was "the young kid on the block." Most of the other nearby college presidents were older; Paul was the youthful innovator who was willing to shake things up and do things differently, for the good of the students.

David Doughty, Christopher Newport's venerable provost, was another early skeptic regarding President Trible. Dave is an enthusiastic, voluble, energetic, and brilliant academic. He came to CNU in 1984, after studying physics at Rutgers Camden as a commuter student, MIT, and then finishing his doctorate in physics at the University of Pennsylvania. He loved the priority of the teacher-student relationships at CNU, as well as the potential for doing collaborative work with particle physics at what would become the Jefferson Lab, which had just arrived in town back in the mid-eighties.

Dave heard the complaints as people worried that Paul was going to elevate the school to the point that it was beyond the reach of local residents. "He wasn't an academic. Sometimes he ruffled feathers. Including mine." One stops to wonder what Dave Doughty would look like with ruffled feathers in his luxuriant mustache, but as Cindi Perry explains, "Dave was part of a senior group of faculty members who were here because we were a commuter campus that focused on part-time, mostly older students. Paul was rejecting that. They had built their time here on a dream that was not Paul's dream. And there was consternation that Paul was not a PhD. Meanwhile another state university was aggressively pursuing the Peninsula, setting up satellite classes in our area. There were rumors that they were going to take us over, and Christopher Newport would no longer exist.

"Back in mid-'90s," she continues, "I don't know how conscious faculty and staff really were that our school was threatened. There were people in government saying, 'Does the Commonwealth of Virginia really need 15 public universities?' We were vulnerable."

But that early stress abated as Paul delivered on what he said he would do, assisted in his great quest by Bill Brauer, who, like Cindi Perry, was one of his earliest "co-conspirators." Bill served as Paul's executive vice president, and would work with him for 25 years until Bill's retirement in 2020.

As a college student in the 1970s, Bill had transferred from Virginia Tech to Christopher Newport. (Tech was just too big and impersonal for his taste, and his dad was Christopher Newport's rector.) Bill went on to get his MBA at the College of William & Mary. He worked in accounting with a Big Six firm but hated the constant travel that took him away from his wife and young family. He took a position at Christopher Newport in early 1992 as vice president for administration and finance, working closely with President Tony Santoro.

Bill was very loyal to Tony, but had understood "when the Board in its wisdom decided it was time for a change" in presidents. He saw that Paul Trible was a person who could clearly and persuasively articulate mission, vision, and values. He wanted to surround himself with people who knew how to get things done, who could translate ideas into action.

"There was a lot of skepticism," he says. "So Paul would tell people, 'If you're unhappy here, you can go and be unhappy somewhere else.'"

Bill had seen people's tendencies to hire people like themselves. CNU had had a less-than-positive ethos for years, and as Bill puts it, the administration had consequently been hiring unhappy people. Yes, there were talented professors and small classes. But the atmosphere was less than a "can-do" sort of place. Students had to wait in interminable lines to register for classes. The financial aid office did not get around to issuing students' checks until September, after classes had already started. The administrative offices closed at the stroke of 5 p.m. If you called with a problem before then, you ended up on hold for a lifetime and treated with a negligible amount of urgency.

Paul brought an energetic positivism that resonated with similarly minded people already at Christopher Newport. He recognized them and formed alliances. He looked to hire people with spirit...people who really cared about making this a great university, people who could provide excellent customer service for generations of students to come. He wasn't interested in naysayers or those who could or would not embrace positive change.

As Bill Brauer sums up the tension in his kind and understated way, "It took a while to get through this transition."

Others were less courteous. Early on, after Paul's first "State of the University" speech, one resident curmudgeon and department head had let it be known that he thought Paul should be doing something practical like improving the library or hiring more professors, rather than painting the grass green and engaging in panoramic rhetoric. As the meeting ended, he left the building with a group of fellow faculty members, muttering his take on the whole thing. "That guy is crazy as hell!"

Paul laughed when the curmudgeon, who eventually became a friend and ally, told him that story. Paul didn't care what anybody called him. He just wanted to make his vision for Christopher Newport into a reality.

CHAPTER 7

SEEING AROUND CORNERS

"The only thing worse than being
blind is having sight but no vision."

— *HELEN KELLER*

"If I give CNU a million bucks, it looks
like two million bucks. If I give it to [an-
other state school], it looks like $500,000."

—*A VIRGINIA LEGISLATOR,
AT A CNU FOOTBALL GAME*

R osemary Trible, who has known Paul the longest, says that "he
sees around corners." This is a valuable superpower; sadly, it's
not really something one can decide to develop. You either have it
or you don't. Great entrepreneurs do, those visionaries who can
see cultural changes coming and anticipate what they will mean for
the marketplace.

Great adventurers have it, like Sir Edmund Hillary and his fellow
climber Tenzing Norgay. They saw themselves at the summit of the
planet's unclimbed, highest mountain. Then in May of 1953, despite

near-impossible obstacles, they stood at the top of Mt. Everest, taking in the view from the "roof of the world."

Perhaps Christopher Newport himself had it: commanding a fleet full of settlers across the choppy Atlantic Ocean in 1607, and establishing them in a New World, is not the lifestyle of someone operating according to the status quo. It's that ability to sense trends before they happen, or to see a daring picture in one's mind of something whole and good when others see only rocks, rubble, and trouble.

As we've said, when Paul first arrived at Christopher Newport, there was a bit of an inferiority complex hanging over the place. His first task as its leader was to dispel that limited and gloomy identity. He did so with relentless positivism that might have worn out a different sort of person. He saw CNU as a winner, and that vision became infectious.

Back when legendary quarterback Tom Brady left the New England Patriots to go to the Tampa Bay Buccaneers, the Bucs were not exactly brimming with optimism about their future. They had missed the playoffs for 12 consecutive years. They had potential but couldn't follow through. They had great veteran players, some rising stars, and talented coaches. "They just needed a quarterback who could elevate them, a leader who could show them the way," *USA Today* editorialized.[vi]

"One of the most important traits Brady learned in New England was the importance of patience, discipline and consistency. Each unit, each player was charged with focusing on his job and finding ways to perfect his craft, and if he did that, improvement would come."

But Brady did more than set a tone with his work ethic and perseverance. As the team improved and went on to the Super Bowl, he started sending text blasts to his teammates. All week, leading up to the big game, around 11 p.m., here came the Brady texts pinging away on the players' cell phones. "We will win this game. We will do it!"

Running back Leonard Fournette said, "Knowing his resume, understanding why he wins…He made us believe."

After their blowout Superbowl victory over the Kansas City Chiefs, the Buccaneers' owner summed it up: "My father had an expression: you wanna know the road ahead, ask the person who's been there. We found that person."

USA Today concluded, "Mission accomplished. Brady delivered. He showed the Bucs how to win, gave them reason to believe and together, they prevailed." Whether you love, hate, or could not care less about Tom Brady, the point is clear.

A visionary leader gives his or her team a vision of what success looks like, as well as the confidence to believe that the team can achieve it.

As you might guess, Paul is fond of Brady's example. "It wasn't his play," Paul says, "but his state of mind. Leaders must wear their vision like the clothes on their backs. You must convince the team that they can be champions."

Still, the vision must be clear, compelling, and winsome enough to be contagious. One person can't carry it alone. The authors of *The Undergraduate Experience: Focusing Institutions on What Matters Most* write,

"In strong institutions, leaders at all levels share a sense of vision and purpose. Those at the top of the organizational chart are crucial actors, but colleges and universities cannot thrive over the long term when a single person or a small group carries a disproportionate share of the load. Instead, people throughout the organization need to see themselves as part of the leadership team. This requires everyone to work together to nurture an institutional culture of inclusion, intentionality, and purpose."[viii]

Particularly since COVID-19, talking about "contagion" is not a happy thing. But the reality is that not just viruses, but positive values and behaviors can be passed on in a geometric progression. One person benevolently affects two, the two extend kindness to four, the four reach out to eight, and so on. British writer C. S. Lewis referred to this principle as "the good infection."

Early on at Christopher Newport, Paul Trible consciously insti- tuted small, mundane habits and courtesies that eventually spread exponentially, and now characterize its community. Paul would pick up any trash he saw on the sidewalks. He held the door for everyone. He walked around and got to know people. His office door was open for students.

We all have seen how *negative* behavioral and attitudinal infections can spread. We've been with families where a parent continually sees other people as threats who are up to no good, the weather is always too hot or too cold, the meal wasn't just right, the waiter was an idiot. Those negative outlooks become the default, conditioning members of the community—in this case the rest of the family—to see life's glass as half empty at best. They are no fun to be around.

Sometimes the same phenomenon happens at dinner parties. One person gossips about a person who is not present, then another person piles on, and then another, and soon the whole atmosphere is sour and malicious.

In a much larger spectrum, politicians can start demonizing their opposition, creating an atmosphere of polarized hostility, members of the media join in with negative caricatures and one-dimensional news bites, and soon the entire political landscape is littered with trash and devoid of the robust, healthy civil discourse that the Founders envisioned.

One day many years ago, Paul was walking the green lawns of one of Virginia's most historic and respected universities. Since he's Paul Trible, he tried to catch people's eyes as they passed by. No one looked at him. He got to the door of the student center, where crowds of students were heading in and out. No one held the door for anyone else. It was every person for himself or herself.

Finally, he asked an older student why people didn't seem to greet one another on this fine campus. "The university is a microcosm of the world," the guy told Paul philosophically. "If you were walking the streets of New York City, no one would speak to you. That's just how the world is."

Paul thanked him and moved on, but as he often tells students and anyone else who will listen, "I thought, 'how sad is that?' Here at Christopher Newport, we are not interested in how the world is. We are interested in the way the world *should be*. We are not interested in conforming to the world; we are interested in transforming the world."

CHAPTER 8

CATANDO DI UN SOGNO

(SINGING OF A DREAM)

"The best way to make your dreams come true is to wake up."
— *PAUL VALERY*

P rovost Dave Doughty likes to make the distinction between being a visionary and being a dreamer. Dave says, consider an author like Jules Verne, who wrote a science fiction novel called *Twenty Thousand Leagues Under the Seas* in the late 1800s. Verne imagined a complex underwater adventure starring a vessel called the Nautilus, which presaged modern submarines.

But Jules Verne did not go on to invent and produce a submarine. It's one thing to have a dream. It's another to make it real.

"Visionaries not only foresee the 'not yet but possible,'" Dave says, "they make it a *reality*. That's the case with Paul and CNU."

One of the most audacious visions Paul had in his early days at Christopher Newport was a picture that popped into his head in the shower before that first budget meeting in Richmond, just a few months after he became president. That image in Paul's mind is the best single example of the whole of what he has done at CNU. It was a bold idea, obviously impossible to pull off, ridiculously ambitious for a small, struggling, little-known university.

But that is the point. Paul's idea did not rest on the common perception of Christopher Newport back in 1996. It grew out of a vision of what CNU could become.

The picture that had come in Paul's head in that shower was a world-class performing arts center on Christopher Newport's campus. It would be an architectural statement that would change the cityscape in mid-town Newport News. It would have theaters, an acoustically perfect concert hall, classrooms, galleries, and could host international stars from around the world. It would be a home for the arts that the entire community could take pride in. Though the idea of an arts center had been discussed by community leaders in the past, it had seemed too ambitious, and had been set aside. There was no cultural center in the entire Peninsula area; this would create a beautiful boost for the community, and a natural bridge between CNU and its neighbors.

Paul had emerged from the shower, rubbed the water out of his eyes, and kept that winsome picture in his mind. During his first visit to Virginia's capitol in Richmond to lobby for money for the university, he pitched the idea to Alan Diamonstein, who, with his wife Beverly, was a great supporter of the arts. As mentioned, the General Assembly appropriated five million dollars in seed money for the project, which would cost—Paul thought—about $20 million.

Paul went to the Newport News City Council and painted his vision for them. They bought in, swayed by the fact he already had some momentum. "It's one thing to have a crazy idea," Paul said later. "It's another thing to have a crazy idea and five million dollars to start it." Newport News voted an immediate grant of $650,000 for architectural planning and pledged another $5 million. The local jurisdictions of Hampton, Poquoson, and York County also got on board with financial support.

Christopher Newport put out requests for architectural proposals. One firm that answered was that of I. M. Pei, the man behind such renowned projects as the glass pyramid at the entrance to the Louvre in Paris, the East Building of Washington D.C.'s National Gallery of Art, Boston's John F. Kennedy Library, and Hong Kong's Bank of China.

Christopher Newport brought the various firms to campus, and when Pei's group laid out their design, Paul was astonished. "Why are you interested in doing a project here?" he asked. The answer came back that the firm had always wanted to design something in Virginia because of the aesthetic and practical challenge of reconciling the colonial history of Virginia with a bold sense of the future.

Paul was ecstatic. Unsurprisingly, however, along with the firm's gorgeous, soaring designs came ever-soaring cost estimates. Committed Christopher Newport friend Robert Freeman and his family gave a million dollars. After an extremely successful business career, Mr. Freeman wanted to benefit others. He told reporters, "We really want do anything we can to give back."

He had become even more positive about the project when he saw the splendor of what the building would be. "I had not planned on giving so much," he said, but when he visited the center as it was under construction and saw the model of the building-to-be, he caught the vision and got excited.[viii] (Mr. Freeman also noted that "it's an expensive proposition to be a friend of Paul Trible's.")

Ferguson Enterprises, based in Newport News, also gave a million dollars. Other corporations and individuals got on board as well. Paul and Rosemary Trible carried the table-top model of the impressive building-to-be around in their car, and enthusiastically used it to encourage many a visionary donor to give.

That architectural model, and the actual building it represented, also inspired students.

Anthony Colosimo, from northern Virginia, was a talented vocal performance high school senior who was considering both Christopher Newport and another, much larger, Virginia state school before his high school graduation in the spring of 2001. He loved CNU's sense of community. He loved that the school awarded him a music scholarship. And he loved that model of the Ferguson Center that by now was on display at the student union. It was a promise of a world-class place for him to hone his craft during his university years.

Anthony came to Christopher Newport in the fall of 2001. He majored in vocal performance and choral music education. CNU's jazz studies program gave him a crossover between different singing styles as part of the curriculum. He sang and acted in Christopher Newport's musicals and plays. He performed various operatic selections. Using the skills he was developing at CNU, he was part of an off-campus award-winning barbershop ensemble called Iguanas in Flight, which is an interesting concept.

When the Ferguson Center opened in 2005, Anthony basically lived in the building, meeting with his professors and vocal coach, spending hours in the practice rooms, and working as a house manager for the performing arts center.

The center launched in phases. The first big concert featured classic crooner Tony Bennett, who performed in the 450-seat Peebles Theatre. Then the acoustically sensational 1700-seat Diamonstein Concert Hall opened. Broadway's Michael Crawford sang there as the first ticketed show, and Anthony was there for it all.

In early 2005, Paul Trible had spent a long Saturday on Christopher Newport's campus at various meetings and events. He came home that evening exhausted, and he and Rosemary sat down with a glass of wine and a tray of cheese and crackers in front of the TV. On screen was a PBS production. It was a concert in Europe featuring an Italian tenor who happened to be blind. Paul stared at the screen. The tenor's voice soared, it flowed. It was like liquid gold.

"Who is this singer?" he asked Rosemary. "THIS is the singer we must have for the Ferguson Center's inaugural concert!"

The tenor's name was Andrea Bocelli.

Paul being Paul, the next thing the Newport News community knew, world-renowned tenor Andrea Bocelli was coming to Christopher Newport.

Everyone asked Paul, "How in the world do you get one of the most prestigious singers in the world to come to CNU?"

"The answer is simple," Paul would say. "Great dreams and the creation of a world-class performing arts center have power and consequence."

He'd pause, then add, "It also helps if you pay the guy a half million dollars."

Tickets for the inaugural concert went for $300, $500, and $1000, except for 200 tickets allotted to CNU students. They were 25 bucks.

Andrea Bocelli and his now-wife, manager, and entourage spent three days in Virginia. The day before the concert, a Wednesday, there was a luncheon in Williamsburg celebrating Mr. Bocelli and the donors and friends who had made the Ferguson Center—and all it represented—possible. As a recipient of the National Italian American Foundation music scholarship, Anthony Colosimo was also there.

During lunch, the effervescent Rosemary Trible sat next to Mr. Bocelli. His English was flawless. She mentioned that Christopher Newport's chamber choir would be performing in Italy the following March. At Andrea's request, Rosemary went and fetched Anthony, who was president of the choir. "Mr. Bocelli was incredibly gracious," Anthony says today. "He asked what I was studying, what I planned to do, and where our choir was going to go in Italy."

"'I would love to hear your choir sing,'" said Andrea Bocelli.

Anthony, an enthusiastic and confident person, responded immediately. "We'd love to sing for you!"

Andrea invited the choir to come to the dress rehearsal that night. They sat in the mezzanine as the entire Virginia Symphony filled the stage, led by the conductor who had accompanied Andrea from Italy.

Andrea's manager approached the group. "I am sorry," he said. "There is just not room on the stage for all of you."

"But," he continued, "which one of you spoke with Mr. Bocelli earlier?"

Anthony raised his hand.

"Mr. Bocelli would like you to perform. Can you sing something?"

Anthony had looked at the concert program. One of the songs

Andrea Bocelli was going to sing was a piece Anthony had performed for his recital the year before. "La Serenata," by Tosti. He knew it well.

"I know that song," he said.

"Excellent," said the manager. "Come."

Anthony got up. "I was freaking out," he says. "I was wearing a pair of khaki pants and a polo shirt. I looked like a dweeb. There were maybe 50 people in the whole concert hall. About seven or eight rows back Mr. Bocelli and his girlfriend sat with the Tribles."

As if he was in a dream, Anthony made it onto the stage. His training kicked in. He could do this. He nodded to the conductor. The symphony launched the opening bars of the music. He sang it. And he nailed it.

His friends in the choir applauded, the symphony members all tapped their feet in affirmation, and then Anthony stood for a moment, not quite sure if he needed to be dismissed or if he should just exit the stage. He could see the Tribles and Andrea Bocelli talking together. He waited.

Andrea Bocelli stood up. "Ah," he said. "Will you sing that in the concert tomorrow night?"

Yes. *Yes!*

Anthony made his way back to his seat, his friends high fiving him all the way. He got hold of his voice coach. He thanked God that his tux, ever ready for a performance, was clean and hanging in his closet. One of his music professors alerted Anthony's parents, three hours away, to this exciting development; Paul invited them to sit with Rosemary and him in the presidential box.

Anthony had assumed that he would just stand next to Andrea Bocelli and sing a line or two of the song, or perhaps harmonize with Mr. Bocelli while the great tenor sang it. But no.

On the evening of October 20, 2005, the Ferguson Center of Christopher Newport University was awash in lights. The marble hallways clicked with high heels and polished dress shoes. The concert hall carried the scent of fine perfumes. There were patrons of the arts from all over Virginia, and international guests as well. The music itself would hang in the air of the concert hall; the acoustics were perfect.

Andrea Bocelli had called for Anthony to come to his dressing room before the performance. Anthony entered to find the tall, handsome Italian relaxing and playing a trumpet. He set it aside. "I am excited to share the stage with you tonight," he told Anthony.

An hour later, the moment came. Anthony walked onto the stage. Andrea waited for him, then stepped back two paces as the orchestra began to play. Anthony looked out over the glittering crowd, and sang as he had been taught to sing, concentrating on the music itself, doing what he loved to do.

As Anthony's final note faded away, there was a moment, then 1700 people jumped to their feet with a massive standing ovation. Andrea Bocelli smiled and clapped as well, still giving Anthony space, not encroaching on his moment.

Overwhelmed, Anthony bowed, thanked Andrea Bocelli, and left the stage.

Today Anthony Colosimo is in his late thirties. He is married and has three small children. He has had a fulfilling career as a music teacher, a vocal performer, and a barbershop ensemble coach. He loves his work. He looks back at his time at Christopher Newport, and that unforgettable weekend in 2005, with a great deal of affection.

"CNU taught me that the people around you matter. I wasn't alone. The faculty, the Tribles, the student body in the music theater department, the administrators...we were all a community of people who cared about one another. The school was small enough that if something didn't exist, you could make it up, and you'd have support to do so. That attitude propelled my professional direction and confidence."

Paul Trible loves to tell the Andrea Bocelli and Anthony Colosimo story to students, though he usually adds a few embellishments.

"I tell students that we are given many opportunities in our lives, if we have eyes to see them. We can seize those moments if we dare to. Anthony had prepared for that moment of opportunity, and he had the courage to embrace it. I can't promise you center stage with Andrea Bocelli, but I can promise you, you *will* have those moments of great opportunity in your life. You must be prepared for those moments—and you must dare to seize them."

CHAPTER 9

IF YOU BUILD IT, THEY WILL COME

"Paul demands excellence but expects miracles."

— *BILL BRAUER*

T he most public aspects of any university tend to be its arts programs and its athletic teams. People from the community get a glimpse into what's going on at the school when they see its students perform, create, or compete in sports arenas. They get swept up into school spirit, or excited about what the students are producing there. (It's harder to create exciting programs that showcase for the public just what is happening in "Advanced Differential Equations," "Digital Signal Processing," or "Environmental Ethics" to pick a few random math, engineering, or philosophy courses.)

So, as we've seen, the Ferguson Center became Christopher Newport's showcase for the arts, and a natural way for people from all over Virginia, and beyond, to enjoy the campus.

A few years prior to that, CNU became, for the first time in its institutional life, a place where people could flock to football games on sunny Saturdays in the fall. And football, as well as the other sports programs, became a catalyst for community solidarity and excitement.

Matt Kelchner came to Christopher Newport in June 2000 to be head coach for the mighty CNU Captains. Great things lay ahead. The only challenge was that the mighty Captains football team did not yet exist.

"It was just me," Matt says today. "I sat down with my wife and made a list of all the things I needed to do to start a football team. Everything. We needed socks. Lockers. Footballs. Uniforms. Goal posts. A field. Coaches. Players. Laundry detergent."

There were 3000 items on Matt's first list.

Matt was a good man for a challenge. He'd grown up in a family of four kids in rural Pennsylvania. His dad was a teacher who went on to become a football coach and a college president. Athletics, hard work, discipline, and academics were all important in the Kelchner household.

Matt played every sport at his high school, and went on to play football and run track at Pennsylvania's Susquehanna University. He loved football and loved coaching. After graduation he chopped firewood and poured concrete to make ends meet so he could take on unpaid coaching jobs. Then he landed a coaching job at Dickinson College; it paid a stipend of $1000. Matt would work the 11 p.m. to 7 a.m. shift at a Denny's Restaurant, drive over to the college with the scent of bacon grease and hash browns in his clothes, sleep in his car for a few hours, and then start his coaching day with his players.

One morning Matt woke up to find a mailbox situated on the hood of his car. When he got to practice, his players were all excited. "Well, Coach," they said. "Every home needs a mailbox, so we got you one!"

Matt ended up eventually moving on to the College of William & Mary in Virginia, where he lived in a real house and coached for 16 years. Then he heard that Christopher Newport University had a crazy new president who was starting a football program. Intrigued, Matt jumped in his car and headed to CNU. He read the entire football feasibility study that had been commissioned. He walked around campus and talked with students and faculty. He read up on Paul Trible's background. And when he met with Paul, he liked "the fact that he was straightforward and honest, no bull." He also liked the fact that the school intended to remain at the Division III level, that there would be no sports scholarships, no "pay to play" aspect at CNU, and that academics really were the priority at Christopher Newport.

Matt loved what football can bring to a university and its community. It draws people together, creates school spirit, brings alumni and neighbors to campus. "I felt that Paul had a good vision of what he wanted to do; I felt like his goals were honorable."

For his part, Paul's expectations for Matt were clear.

1. The players were to graduate on time.
2. The players were to be *student* athletes, putting academics first. If there was a choice between completing a chemistry lab and being late to practice, the priority was to finish the chem lab.
3. The program was to have a positive social impact on the university.
4. The players were to put the team first, above their individual interests.
5. And they had to win.

Matt had 16 months from his hiring to his first game. The first business at hand was to find some players. (Thankfully, the stadium was already under construction, helped along by gifts from local auto dealership POMOCO, which maintained naming rights for 17 years. Today the stadium is named for TowneBank.)

One of the conditions of Matt's hiring was that he'd asked Paul Trible to help him recruit. Matt knew that Newport News and its surrounding areas would be a great hunting ground for players, and he started bringing them to campus. Paul showed up to meet them, and other staff and faculty joined in to talk about Christopher Newport's rigorous academic programs and the great help they would receive to be successful in both their classes and their sport. Matt had to recruit about 600 large young men to get 100 players to actually come to CNU, but he did it. In December of that year, he was able to hire three coaches to give him a hand.

Incredibly, when September 1, 2001 rolled around, Christopher Newport was ready to play some football. The stadium didn't yet have a press box or all its bleachers in place, but the new field was one of the finest grass playing surfaces in the South, and the players were pumped up.

It rained all that morning, but the stadium was full of 6,135 cheering students and people from the community. Standing room only. A helicopter from the local news outlet, WAVY, appeared in the distance over the stadium. The helicopter circled, landed, and yes, Captain Chris, the CNU mascot, complete with his swirling blue cape, fedora with plume, and dashing mustache, hopped out to deliver the game ball before the playing of the National Anthem.

The fans went wild.

It wasn't yet a Cinderella story, however.

Christopher Newport lost that first game, 21 – 6. And their second. Matt was disappointed, but not surprised; his guys had never played together as a team.

They battled hard in the third game, but lost in overtime.

By the fourth game, which was in North Carolina, Matt saw the members of the opposing team yukking it up, taking a group photo as they came onto the field. He gathered his guys. "Do you see that?" he said. "They're talking trash. They have no respect for us."

Matt's players got fired up. And they won.

After that, the CNU Captains just got better and better. They won the following game. And the next, and the next. After one home victory, as the fans rushed the field, Matt saw his 300-pound center, Tommy Fitzgerald, heading for Rosemary Trible, who was jumping up and down with excitement. Tommy swept Rosemary up and swung her around and around, high in the air. Matt Kelchner saw Rosemary's little feet flying by in a blur, everyone laughing and congratulating one another, and felt good. They'd done it.

That season, Christopher Newport University became the first team in NCAA history to go to the post-season playoffs in their first year of existence. They went back to the playoffs the next year. And the next. And the next.

Matt's 3000-item list had paid off.

Scott Millar was just one alum who was first drawn back into Christopher Newport because of the football program. He and his wife Muriel are ardent football fans, love tailgating parties, and have been at just about every home game for more than 20 years.

Scott went to Ferguson High School before it was incorporated into Christopher Newport's campus. He wasn't sure what he wanted to do, had two cousins who were on the Christopher Newport faculty, and ended up coming to CNU in 1981. He majored in government administration, minored in history, and graduated in 1985. He went on to work in human resources in the city government, then went on in 1992 to become a human resources executive at Canon Virginia, headquartered in Newport News. Today Scott serves as senior vice president and general manager of the human resources, audit, ethics, and business consultation divisions at the digital imaging corporate giant Canon USA in New York. As an alumnus, community, and business leader with a love for the university, Scott has served on CNU's Board of Visitors and as its rector.

His business savvy informs his analysis of Christopher Newport's trajectory over the decades since he was a student there.

Scott says that Christopher Newport in its early years had been a model of the professional education commuter experience. The school had few traditional students; many were working full-time and needed a college education to advance their positions. Many had families. Many were veterans taking classes on the GI bill.

By the mid-1990s, Scott says that model needed to change because the environment was changing. Technology was on the rise, along with online enrollment. Military bases were offering remote classes on base. And nearby community colleges were offering a mix of online classes and more convenient scheduling.

At the same time, Christopher Newport was not strongly supported by the General Assembly, so funding was an issue. It didn't have a pipeline of new students. Its mission had become outdated, and its enrollment numbers were falling. It was facing a disruption in the market, so to speak. It would have to adapt and change to survive, just as any company adapted, say, to the enormous disrupter of Covid, or like companies in Scott's field had to adapt after the disruption of digital technology shook up the world of film.

In short, for Christopher Newport to continue in the changing market, it had to find its niche. It was a classic case of the need for disruptive innovation. To survive, the university needed a visionary leader who could create a new brand in the marketplace. As disruptive innovation theory holds, such leaders are generally entrepreneurs, outsiders, and idealists rather than industry insiders.

So when Scott heard Paul Trible talk about Christopher Newport as a residential, liberal arts school with high academic focus, small class size, and 5000 students in a premiere public university setting, he got it. He believed that Paul was accurately seeing powerful, positive changes that could happen in CNU and its broader community... if people got on board to invest in making the vision a reality.

It wasn't just the physical makeover of the place. Scott says, "It's one thing to transform the campus with buildings and great architecture; it's another to transform the people who are housed here. In developing the leadership program, Paul was recruiting the Eagle Scouts of the world, the young leaders who would bring that attitude to campus. Today you can see the character and the values of Christopher Newport students who are working in the community. They have high character. Honesty. Empathy and an appreciation for the humanity of others. Those are the values of a leader."

For many years, Scott would bring groups of Canon's executive team to Newport News, where they could tour Canon's manufacturing operation and participate in a multi-day retreat.

One evening at dinner, Scott invited Paul to speak to the group about his views on transformational leadership and how its effects had played out at Christopher Newport. Paul told the assembled executives that the sense of vision and values had penetrated the atmosphere there, so every "customer," or student, could tell you the secret sauce of CNU.

"You can walk across our campus," he told the group, "And any student can tell you exactly what I've been saying. They know what a 'life of significance' means, and are challenged to pursue it."

There was some pushback. The execs were dubious that 18 to 22-year-olds would readily absorb Trible's shiny vision.

The group was staying at a local Marriott property. The next morning, they were all eating breakfast at adjacent tables at the hotel's restaurant. It turned out that their cheerful server was a student at Christopher Newport.

"So," said one of the guys, "Tell me about CNU's vision and values..."

Holding her coffee pot, the girl stopped. "Well, it's not like I have some big organizational analysis for you. All I know is that at CNU, people matter. I know we try to pursue excellence in everything. Like waiting tables. I know we need to serve others who are less fortunate. And I know that wherever I go from CNU, I want to live a life of significance. I want to do stuff that really matters."

Then she went on to serve her other tables.

Paul Trible doesn't use words like "stuff," but it was clear that this random student had caught the vision. Scott Millar told Paul later that the Canon executives had all looked at each other and figured that Christopher Newport must be doing something right. "Throughout the rest of those meetings, that waitress was a guiding light, that CNU was not just a place of impressive buildings, but of impressive people."

In 2000, while CNU's football stadium was under construction, a local businessperson named Gary Minter was visiting Paul's offices with several executive colleagues from POMOCO, the auto dealership business that had given generously to make the new stadium a reality in its early years.

Today, well more than two decades later, Gary remembers looking up at the wall in Paul Trible's office. There was an immense architectural rendering of the university's overall plan, with drawings of every building not yet built lining the perimeters of long, generous lawns and classic bricked plazas. "It's unbelievable," Gary says. "Some schools have all kinds of architecture added over the years as needs arise. But from the beginning, Paul had a plan. It showed every single building. They were all classically beautiful. And he followed through."

Early on, Paul worked with Glavé and Holmes, the Richmond firm that has designed many of the most beautiful buildings in Virginia, at universities, resorts, historic places, and upscale estates all over the Commonwealth. Paul liked the firm's philosophy, as summed up by Randy Holmes, "There is no question we are in unprecedented times of rapid change and technological advancement. Our needs, however, for a sense of place and meaningful connections to the community...have not changed. Understanding this...has historically informed the structures of our civic life, individual liberties, and the architect's role in expressing them." So the firm uses "the fundamental and timeless principles of harmony, rhythm, proportion, beauty, and human scale to create buildings...that address people's desire for connection and that evoke enjoyment and appreciation of one's own place in the world."[ix]

As they sought to remove the old structures and to create pillared places of beauty on Christopher Newport's campus, Paul and Executive Vice President and Chief Finance Officer Bill Brauer knew that they could not rely *solely* on the state funding of building projects as that, in Bill's words, would "take forever."

Christopher Newport, like most institutions of higher learning, already had an education foundation, a nonprofit corporation that fostered its mission. But CNU was a young school, compared to those that had been around for generations and had hundreds of thousands of alumni. Christopher Newport had far fewer alumni, and many had not yet gained the kind of wealth that older donors tend to give to their alma maters. Paul and Bill considered the challenge, and in June 1997 created, with others, CNU's Real Estate Foundation, a nonprofit corporation functioning as a holding and management company. It allowed the university to acquire nearby properties, and to build many of Christopher Newport's beautiful residential buildings over the years, even as state monies continued to fund other campus construction projects.

As the university identified properties, the real estate foundation would borrow the money, buy the property, build the building, and then the university would lease it back from the foundation, which would use those funds to pay principal and interest. The foundation became one of the most important vehicles in the creation of the new CNU. It allowed the administration to buy properties and expand the campus quickly, and to create residential facilities that would draw students to come to Christopher Newport.

The foundation also served as a vehicle for business and community leaders to get involved with the university. Many who had supported Paul in his political life were now getting excited about Christopher Newport's tremendous potential under his leadership. As they served on the foundation's board and employed their experience and expertise to advise and give lift to Christopher Newport, they would get more involved, and become champions for the university.

Bill Brauer notes that CNU's was one of the first such real estate foundations in the Commonwealth of Virginia; over the years, many other universities came to CNU to learn how to create one. By the start of the 2021-2022 school year, the market value of Christopher Newport's Real Estate Foundation was more than $220 million.

Christopher Newport's overall plan prioritized facilities for students. The first to go up was the Freeman Center, a sports and convocation center and the home to CNU's intercollegiate basketball, volleyball, and track and field programs, as well as a place where students could work out, run on the indoor track, play intramural sports, and hang out together. Then there were the first of the residence halls—James

River Hall and York River Hall, as well as the Christopher Newport University Apartments—comfortable living spaces where students would actually want to reside, a far cry from the hot cinderblock boxes that many of their parents recalled from their own college days.

A few years later came the David Student Union, which would become a center of student life—and dining—on campus. The Ferguson Center for the Performing Arts, a cultural center for students and community alike.

A baseball stadium. Then the gorgeous library...and then, once these main student magnets, as well as other improvements, were in the pipeline, academic buildings started rolling out, as well as everything from tennis courts, a soccer stadium, a bell tower, chapel, a non-sexy but ever-popular parking deck, gates, statues, an alumni house, Greek village, and the spectacular Torggler Fine Arts Center, a masterpiece of marvelous teaching venues, soaring public spaces, and galleries designed for the exhibition of world-class art.

As the beautiful buildings went up, and students and parents visited campus, enrollments went up as well. Paul was often on the road with Christopher Newport admission officers all over Virginia, meeting students, listening to parents, and, in his inimitable way, painting word pictures for them to visualize themselves at Christopher Newport University.

"This is not the university for everyone," he'd say. "But we are a caring community where you'll be a name and not a number. You'll have gifted professors who know your name, inspiring architecture that rivals that of the most beautiful campuses in the nation, an acoustically perfect concert hall, top-of-the-line athletic facilities. You're going to live in the greatest residence halls in America, enjoy brand-new sports facilities, exceptional dining halls, a tremendous library..." The list went on and on.

"Paul branded the university for what it was and what it was becoming," Bill Brauer says. "And when young people actually came to campus, then they would fall in love. Not only with the surroundings, but with who they might become if they came to college here."

Every interest group wanted their particular building prioritized, but Paul and his team kept their hands steady on the tiller. There was a clear order in which things would roll out.

Scott Millar says, "One thing I've always admired in Paul's leadership is his ability to say 'no' in a very effective way. That's really hard in higher education. When you have someone willing to write a check with a lot of zeroes, it's hard to turn that down. He has stuck to his vision and has been able to have successes so people can see why he is prioritizing in a certain way."

Scott points out that there was a group of Christopher Newport grads who were very anxious to have an alumni house on campus. "Paul was very polite, but the timing was not right. All would come in due time." Paul had a strategic plan in his rollout of infrastructure, and current students' needs would take priority over those who had preceded them.

Much of this development would not have been possible without acquiring more property on which to build.

When Paul arrived at Christopher Newport, the campus was situated in a residential neighborhood, as it had been since 1961. Bordered by Warwick Boulevard, it was hidden by gas stations, run-down apartments, and small businesses. Forty thousand cars a day flowed up and down Warwick Boulevard, and many of their occupants had no idea that they were driving past a university. It was just as well. Christopher Newport's buildings, erected in a time whose architecture was often characterized by angular, minimalist design and exposed concrete, did not necessarily please the eye.

Over the years, the Real Estate Foundation was able to buy up properties that were adjacent to the campus as they became available. Or Paul, Bill, and Cindi would meet with homeowners, inquire about any plans to move, and make generous offers.

One such neighbor was the Reverend Marcellus Harris, a warm, hearty, and bigger-then-life leader in the African American community. Marcellus' home and church, First Baptist Morrison, were both on property that is now part of CNU's campus.

Before Paul Trible arrived at Christopher Newport, as it became clear that change was coming to the community, Marcellus had been disappointed in communications with the school. "We didn't particularly trust what we were being told" by the university, he says today.

When Paul took CNU's helm in 1996, Marcellus already knew of him from his service in Congress. "Paul already had a great reputation in the African American community. And then he came [to CNU] and created an atmosphere of trust and a relationship with us. He developed a friendship. He said he would help us—and he did everything that he said he would do."

"Paul was genuine," Marcellus continues, smiling. "He and Rosemary would come to our church. He fell right into line with our worship; he wasn't an oddball at all!" (Strong praise coming from a Black Baptist about a White Episcopalian.)

Marcellus says that Paul was instrumental in making sure the church was well-reimbursed for its properties, and in helping Marcellus find a great, seven-acre piece of land for his church to relocate, "leaving us in better shape than we were before."

That move was, of course, many years ago. Marcellus retired as pastor of First Baptist Morrison in 2016 after 45 years as its leader. He says that his friendship with the Tribles continues to this day. "They've had us for Christmas parties; we get together for dinner when we can. My wife and I consider Paul and Rosemary the dearest and most faithful of friends."

It's clear that Christopher Newport's leadership did not regard the acquisition of properties as just a bloodless business expansion. It was, as it is today, all about relationships and giving lift not only to the university, but to the entire community it serves.

Today, when he looks back at those years of almost-constant-construction, Bill Brauer laughs and says, "Over the years we acquired 120 properties. We couldn't have done it today. It was all about timing. The economy in Virginia was booming back then. If interest rates had not been as low as they were, or if construction costs were not as low...we could not have accomplished what we did."

Bill, like Scott Millar, also sees that the timing was ripe in the marketplace for an entrepreneurial leader like Paul to bring change. "We were collectively at a point we knew something needed to happen," he says. Though there was plenty of pushback, there was also a sense that Christopher Newport had to change, or it would not survive. The time was right for a thick-skinned and visionary leader to chart a bold course and move forward quickly.

"Yes," says retired Chief of Staff Cindi Perry. "For years, the joke was that you could leave campus for lunch at the middle of the day, come back, and there would be a new building under construction."

CHAPTER 10

PERSEVERING THROUGH CONFLICT

"We must care more than others think is wise, risk more than others think is safe, dream more than others think is practical and expect more than others think is possible."

— VARIOUSLY ATTRIBUTED TO VINCE LOMBARDI, HOWARD SCHULTZ, CADET MAXIM, CLAUDE T. BISSELL, AND UNKNOWN

Years ago, the president of another great Virginia university was writing a book about leadership. She called her friend Paul Trible to interview him about his early days at Christopher Newport, when he was holding forth a grand and glorious vision before a rather skeptical audience.

"You've been a congressman and a senator," she said, alluding to the fact that academia was not his field. "Weren't you concerned about failure?" she asked.

Paul thought about it for a moment. "It never even entered my mind."

Few of us can relate to this type of thinking, but Paul seems to have been blessed with relentless optimism and vigorous self-confidence. It's probably, as his colleagues sometimes tease him, because he was an only child.

Cultivating that positivism is usually part of his speeches to students. He talks about the great Babe Ruth, who struck out 1330 times, yet is remembered as one of the greatest home run hitters of all time. Babe said that "Every strike brings me closer to the next home run."

Inventor Thomas Edison is famously said to have quipped about his lengthy process to capture electricity, "I have not failed. I have just found 1000 ways not to make a light bulb." Sir Winston Churchill, England's inspirational leader during the bleakest days of World War II, when hope seemed dim against Hitler's Nazi scourge, once addressed his alma mater: "Never give in. Never give in. Never, never, never, never—in nothing, great or small, large or petty—never give in, except to convictions of honour and good sense. Never yield to force. Never yield to the apparently overwhelming might of the enemy."

Basketball legend Michael Jordan said, "I've missed 9,000 shots in my career. I've lost almost 300 games. Twenty-six times I've been trusted to make the winning shot and I missed. I've failed over and over in my life and that's why I succeed."

Failure, opposition, and distress are endemic to success. Perhaps the most painful failure Paul had to face came when he was a young man. He'd fallen in love with Rosemary; they had met while she was at Sweet Briar College, before she'd transferred to the University of Texas at Austin to pursue her dream of broadcast communications. Their relationship had grown deep, even though they were far apart in miles, and this was back in a day without cell phones or FaceTime.

Paul was ready to propose. He traveled to Austin with a small velvet box in his pocket. He and Rosemary were to spend a romantic afternoon out on beautiful Lake Travis; Paul had rented a small boat for the occasion. He rowed far from shore, letting the little craft drift gently in the tranquil, blue waters.

He somehow managed to kneel without capsizing the boat. He presented the velvet box and the ring. He asked Rosemary to be his wife.

She declined.

It wasn't that she had doubts about Paul, it was just that she wanted to pursue her broadcast career, and she felt that the timing was not right. Still, as you can imagine, it was an awkward conversation.

Paul stuffed the box back in his pocket and rowed the damn rowboat all the way back to the shore in the blazing Texas sun. He dejectedly returned to Virginia.

Within just a few weeks, Rosemary had a change of mind. She called her beloved. "Do you still have that fuzzy velvet box?" she asked. He did.

So they became engaged.

Christopher Newport students love to hear this story. It fascinates them that P. Tribs, as they fondly call President Trible, once actually had to face a failure—albeit brief—in his visionary life.

His love story had a happy ending, but Paul often tells students that there is particular pain in the calling to be a leader. "Courage is absolutely essential to leadership because you have to step forward and often stand alone," he told graduate students from Elon University's Master of Arts in Higher Education, who focused on Christopher Newport's transformation as a case study in 2021. "You have to bring new ideas. You have to make change and there is a creative tension in all of this. People do not like change. They resist it.

"Not only does change generate resistance and criticism, but leaders will often fall flat on their faces and have their ideas rejected. And that hurts. Leadership requires a tough hide and a short memory. In politics you learn that people who are your allies today can be adversaries tomorrow, and vice versa. You have to build bridges, and you have to have a vision that is so powerful that you can ignore the doubters. You have to have a 'yes' that is so compelling that you can ignore the naysayers."

During his tenure at Christopher Newport, particularly in the early years, Paul had abundant opportunities to live out his convictions about courage, vision, leadership, and change. It's worth looking back at some of those tough times, though this book is not able to plumb their complexities. The point is that change is hard in the moment, but it can yield great benefits—and deeper relationships—for the long run.

Early on, back in early 2000, his speech to the Christopher Newport faculty gives a window into some of its growing pains as CNU transitioned from its old self-image to the new.

This was four years after Paul became president of the university. He acknowledged that a senior faculty member had admonished him to move away from his usual "pep rally style" and to employ "understatement and avoid hyperbole."

Paul continued. "But when I talk about Christopher Newport that's an impossible task—CNU's story—our story—is magical. Christopher Newport has moved farther faster than any school in the history of Virginia, and perhaps, in the country."

Paul painted the inspiring pictures that he used when he talked about Christopher Newport to high school guidance counselors, parents, potential students, and the state legislature. He then moved into more comfortable turf for the academy: strategic indicators, graphs, and data that showed the remarkable increases in applicants, student retention, grade point averages, new buildings, faculty salaries, credentials, reduced teaching load, and other improvements Christopher Newport had already made during his time there.

He also talked about Christopher Newport's commitment to great teaching and relationships between student and professors; that would remain unchanged. But while the old "model of an urban university, with open admissions, accepting students of all ages and a very large number of part-time students who would come and go" was a very worthy mission, it was "a model that hasn't worked at CNU in over a decade. As we have seen, part-time students have been leaving us in large numbers.

"So, we are evolving a new sense of what we are to become—one of America's preeminent public liberal arts colleges. This vision is absolutely consistent with our tradition and values and our focus on great teaching and small classes and personal attention and the importance of liberal education."

A year later, after the U. S. economy suffered a recession in the spring of 2001, the Commonwealth of Virginia staggered under a budget crisis. Budgets across the state had to be slashed; the General Assembly cut funding to CNU and other state universities by about 25 percent.

This required decisive leadership and bold action. Christopher Newport put together a task force of senior tenured faculty and administrators, chaired by a faculty member, to conduct a study. Other schools cut their budgets across the board. Paul and other leaders realized that doing so would in fact diminish CNU's programming effectiveness across the board.

The task force study revealed that various academic programs were under-performing. The nursing program had already been under consideration; it just was not producing enough graduates each year in comparison to the financial investment it took to run it. In addition, other nearby schools offered nursing degrees; did Christopher Newport need to replicate such programs? The undergraduate degree in physical education, otherwise known as "leisure studies," did not pass scrutiny. Neither did the master's in psychology or the master's program in teaching the way it was structured at that time. These needed to be cut; their professors would have to be let go.

Such reductions were painful, to say the least, particularly since professors in those programs had to finish out their teaching cycles until their students graduated. There was bitter pushback from some students and community members as well.

In the case of the teaching degree, Paul and a group of senior faculty and administrators sought to find a way for the university to continue providing good teachers for the community, and to do so in a method that was more successful and more consistent with the vision to establish Christopher Newport as a first-class institution emphasizing the liberal arts and sciences. That effort gave rise to a five-year program that combined the four-year undergrad degree to gain expertise in one's chosen field—math, history, or whatever—and a one-year master's focus on education that would equip the student for excellence in teaching as a career, with all the certifications required by the Commonwealth. This degree program now serves as a model for the state.

"Leadership is the flowing back and forth of energy and ideas," Paul often says, and this flowing exchange—which initially grew out of conflict—with stakeholders in the community and among alumni, staff, faculty, and students yielded a better program than what had existed before, a program that is flourishing today.

"During that time, Paul was getting hammered," says Cindi Perry. "But he listened, and the conflict in fact led to a new and stronger solution."

Paul Trible doesn't like to talk about conflict. Unlike many of us, he has an uncanny ability to forget it and move on. His wife says that she's marveled during Paul's political career at the way her resilient husband could forgive and forget barbed arrows that political opponents shot at him. At Christopher Newport—a far less contentious environment than Capitol Hill—there is still conflict, strongly held opinions, as there is anywhere you have brilliant, gifted, diverse, opinionated professionals gathered in one community. Any transformational leader encounters dispute; most human beings are just not crazy about disruptive change.

But even if Paul Trible doesn't remember conflict, it's profitable to note a few tussles over the years. Like the example of the master's in education, they illustrate the silver lining of well-conducted disputes in opinion. They can make a body of people stronger together. If a leader is open to a soundly reasoned argument presented with solid supporting data, and he or she is willing to change his or her mind, conflict can lead to creative solutions that are better than what preceded them.

When Cindi Perry looks back at the budget crisis of 2001 and 2002, it was an extremely tough time. "But we came out of it stronger. We came out of it knowing we could survive."

A few years later, the economy boomed. Christopher Newport had a significant increase in its budget and new money the administration could invest to strengthen and deepen its curricula.

One benefit of the lean times, though, was that Christopher Newport's decision to completely cut a few programs rather than trim from all programs built more credibility with the General Assembly. "It was a bold move," says Cindi. "It was really well received. We had a lot of supporters in the legislative staff. They would tell us, 'Your priorities remain the same, year to year to year; other schools come to us with the flavor of the month.'"

Paul's natural skill and political expertise meant that his Richmond visits with legislators were fruitful. He would come in with two or three priority allocations or legislative needs and concentrate his time on the legislators who could help, rather than uniformly visiting all of them, as some college presidents did. "We were so blessed to have Alan Diamonstein in the House appropriations committee and other great allies," says Cindi.

Paul also built good relationships with staffers to the delegates. They were the ones providing the data. Paul treated them as the professionals they were. "I always found that to be a really wonderful thing," says Cindi, "because I had been one of those budget people in the back corner. He gave them professional respect."

One key meeting in Richmond during those early years did not go quite so well, however. One March morning, Cindi drove from her home in Hampton over to Christopher Newport and met Paul and Bob Doane there. Bob was an integral part of their team; he served as CNU's provost for four years and played a decisive role in shaping CNU's growing transformation and success.

They all hopped in Bob's car and sped on to Williamsburg, 30 minutes up the road toward Richmond, to pick up Bill Brauer. After they did so and got underway, Cindi, in the front passenger seat, kept her head turned toward Paul and Bill in the back, engrossed in strategic conversation about their day. Time passed. Plans developed.

Finally, Paul, Bill, and Cindi looked up, expecting to see the buildings of downtown Richmond. Instead, there was the Hampton Coliseum, and they were speeding east, directly toward the Chesapeake

Bay and directly away from Richmond. Intent on the conversation flowing from the back seat, Bob had somehow driven precisely the wrong way on I-64 for 45 minutes, and now they were going to be very late for their morning meetings with legislators.

"To this day we don't know what Bob was thinking," says Cindi. "Paul thought it was hysterical. But it was the last time Bob drove us to the General Assembly."

When Paul does look back at the early, more difficult years of setting Christopher Newport on a new course, he says, "Some faculty and staff had become complacent and resigned to second-class citizenship in the academic world. We had to give those who shared our aspirations the opportunity to contribute to the transformation, and those who did not the opportunity to either adapt or leave.

"Opponents and skeptics could—at first—be found almost everywhere. Many opponents simply feared change of any kind. Skeptics often professed that the new vision was good but unrealizable. Both groups were the targets of concerted outreach efforts. We saw both opponents and skeptics as potential allies and supporters. Today, most of them are."

One such ally is Bill Thomas, who had initially wondered if Paul had the experience in academia to right Christopher Newport's sinking ship. "I watched and learned," he says today. "Paul was clearly a very smart and shrewd individual. In the beginning I did not know if he was just political in his motivations. But I saw him listen to those who disagreed with him. I saw over time that what he was saying was consistent with how he lived his life. And he did what he said he was going to do."

Bill served several terms on Christopher Newport's Board of Visitors. "Paul listens and learns from those who have different points of view. And he has the ability to turn critics into allies."

Quentin Kidd, who has watched Christopher Newport's progress since Paul first took charge, says that today "Most faculty are post-Paul. If he tried to change things now, the faculty would have their pitchforks out."

As Quentin notes, change was also possible because of timing. "Northern Virginia was exploding in population, with middle-class families making good money and looking for good schools where they could send their kids. Paul saw opportunity there, and that we needed lots of changes" to make Christopher Newport a place that students and their parents would choose over other Virginia schools.

Quentin says that people have gotten used to Paul. Success begets success, and Paul has been successful in ways that have muted faculty dissonance or won people over. He raised faculty salaries, and a decade or so ago he lowered the teaching load, with the understanding that this would free faculty to invest more time in each student and to increase the rigor of their academics.

Transformation always brings challenges. Christopher Newport moved through them, and because it is a place that prioritizes people, situations that elicited conflict and change could also bring deeper relationships.

Virginia Purtle offers an example of that. She was a Dean of social sciences and professional studies back in the 1990s. When Paul decided to streamline things in 1996, he cut the number of deans. No one likes to eliminate positions, but he believed the cuts were in the best interest of the university. A local reporter asked Paul about the restructuring, and Paul gave a quote that may well not have been the most sensitive comment he could have shared. He said that Virginia had "worked her heart out," but that "when the music stopped, there was one person left standing."[x]

Gracious in the midst of it all, Virginia was given a semester of paid administrative leave, and then returned to Christopher Newport as a much-loved professor of sociology.

A few years later when some faculty members and students were outraged about something, Virginia quietly reached out to Paul.

As Paul remembers the conversation, she told him that "I have some ideas that might help this situation."

"I'm so grateful," Paul responded. "Can we get together?"

They agreed that it would be better not to meet on campus, so she came over to his home.

As Virginia entered the Tribles' living room, she inadvertently knocked over a glass-topped library table adjacent to the sofa. The glass toppled to the floor and shattered everywhere. Absolutely abashed, she apologized profusely, but Paul and Rosemary, who came rushing in when she heard the crash, were just thankful that Virginia wasn't hurt by the shards of glass.

Oddly enough, the accident broke not only the table, but the tension. Virginia and Paul had an extraordinary, free-flowing conversation. Paul listened carefully to Virginia's perspective. Her insights helped him immensely. The two re-established a strong relationship and continuing, quiet, and honest conversations over the next few years. Paul eventually asked Virginia to become Vice Provost and to lead Christopher Newport's student success programs across the campus.

Virginia Purtle retired in 2007. She was awarded Professor Emeritus status for her many contributions to Christopher Newport. She stopped by the campus for lunch with Paul a year or so ago; they enjoyed the reality of a once-broken relationship restored—and strengthened—because they were willing to listen to one another, grow through conflict, and emerge as friends.

As Bill Brauer says about his 25 years of relationships, particularly in those early years at Christopher Newport—which of course built the foundation for *today's* CNU—"We all liked each other. If we didn't like each other, we would not have been as successful."

CRAZY AS HELL

Freshmen Dessert at the President's Residence, Three Oaks

Students from Christopher Newport College
visit with young Congressman Trible, late 1970s

Rosemary and Paul crown Homecoming royalty, 2017

Hump Day: students on International study in Morocco

New Christopher Newport President Paul Trible puts students first in the most unlikely place: the parking lot

CRAZY AS HELL

BOYD'S EYE VIEW   **BENTLEY BOYD**

Visit Bentley on the World Wide Web, at http://www.dailyxpress.com/boyd/ — or e-mail him at brodyboyd@aol.com

View of President Trible's challenge ahead, Daily Press 1996

Ferguson Center Groundbreaking, April 2002

The 'old' Administration Building when Paul Trible arrived at CNU

Christopher Newport's administration building today, Christopher Newport Hall

The Ferguson Center for the Arts designed by I.M. Pei - opened in 2005

Student Anthony Colosimo and Andrea Bocelli on stage the Ferguson Center

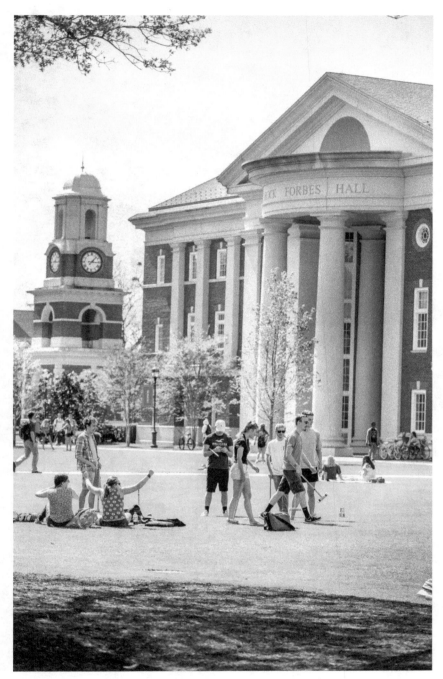

Springtime on campus

The C. Larry and Mary Pope Chapel - opened in 2013

The Mary M. Torggler Fine Arts Center - opened in 2021

The Rosemary Trible Reading Room

Sixty-five percent of classes have less than 19 students in them

Students outside the David Student Union on Greek Bid Day

Annual Day of Service

The Penny Toss at Commencement

Captains lead the way

Always faithful and full of spirit, CNU Blue Crew student fan club

Women's Soccer: Division III National Champions 2021

Paul Trible welcomes a new student on Freshman Move-in Day

Paul Trible and students on the Great Lawn

The joyous dedication of Greek Village, 2016

Rosemary and Paul in 2017

The Great Lawn becomes a busy thoroughfare during class change

The Paul and Rosemary Trible Library - Expansion Ribbon Cutting 2018

Aerial view of the heart of campus - The Great Lawn

Commencement Day!

Trible Tradition: Rosemary congratulates (and offers hugs)
to each graduate after they cross the stage

Paul Trible presides over the Commencement Exercises

"My school is Disney World." - Lawson Herold '21

CHAPTER 11

A CULTURE
OF KINDNESS

"Someday, after mastering the winds, the waves,
the tides and gravity, we shall harness for God the
energies of love, and then, for a second time in the
history of the world, man will have discovered fire."

— *PIERRE TEILHARD DE CHARDIN*

I n 2020, *The Princeton Review* named Christopher Newport University
as one of the nation's best colleges, combining a "superb" education with distinguished career preparation at an affordable cost. *The
Review* cited students' descriptions of CNU as a place with "a culture
of kindness" that cultivates "a sense of expectation." *The Princeton
Review* editors praised Christopher Newport's President's Leadership
Program and Honors Program, its core curriculum in the arts and
sciences, and the commitment of its students to civic engagement
through community service.[xi]

"The schools we name as our Best Value Colleges for 2020 comprise
only seven percent of the nation's four-year colleges," *The Princeton
Review's* editor-in-chief explained. "They are truly distinctive and
diverse in their programs, size, region, and type, yet they are similar

in three areas. Every school we selected offers outstanding academics, generous financial aid and/or a relative low cost of attendance, and stellar career services."

Christopher Newport was one of only four public universities in Virginia (along with William & Mary, University of Virginia, and Virginia Tech) and one of only 63 public universities nationwide to be included in Princeton's list.

These are the kinds of kudos that college recruiters love, with good reason. But the survey's unusual choice of words merits a second look. *A culture of kindness.*

The empathetic focus on the dignity, worth, and unique potential of the individual is so essential to CNU's culture that it hardly needs saying. This mindset springs from the heart of what it means to live a life of significance, to serve and value others as an innate mindset and lifestyle.

Kindness starts, as always, with small things. Early on at Christopher Newport, after Paul had ripped out the administration parking signs in favor of the notion that the *students* are the school's customers, he set a tone. He called it a "speaking tradition," which at first sounds like oratory in the public square, but it's something more personal and elemental.

At Christopher Newport, students are expected to look one another in the eye. They are expected to speak to one another, both to people they know, of course, but more importantly, to people they don't know. Paul Trible says, "if you don't look them in the eye, you are saying 'you don't matter.' And everyone should matter." They are expected to help campus visitors who ask for directions to this building or that. Like the staff at strong customer service businesses, students are expected not to just point out the directions, as in "go that-a-way," but to offer to take the visitor to the place he or she is seeking. And students are expected to hold the door for one another.

These expectations are not autocratic directives from the top. They are what used to be called manners—small courtesies that let others know they are welcome, they are valued, and that they matter. They can't be legislated; they must be inculcated by the habits of the majority of members of a community. They can't be spontaneously apprehended; they must be modeled and caught.

One day Paul Trible was with a group of students walking toward the student union. One guy grabbed the door to hold it for the others in the group. As they made their way through, he looked, and now there was a mob of people heading in his direction, all making their way to the door of the building.

"Uh, President Trible," he asked. "How long *do* I have to hold the door?"

Holding doors is good. Helping weary parents unload their cars on first-year students moving in day is awesome.

Many years ago, when Paul and Rosemary Trible first took their daughter Mary Katherine to college in South Carolina, it was a miserable experience. It was about 100 degrees outside, there were long, sweaty lines of unhappy parents and students waiting for elevators, and the alternative to waiting was schlepping all of Mary Katherine's abundant stuff up seven long flights of concrete stairs.

The Tribles survived, but Paul was determined to find a better experience for both parents and students on Christopher Newport's college move-in day. He recruited members of the football team, faculty, and leadership program, equipped them with big, rolling carts, and came up with a plan. "It's called servant leadership," says Paul. "It's a way to powerfully communicate. It underscores the culture that we have built."

As one happy parent wrote in a letter to the *Daily Press* newspaper, he and his son had expected "that all-too-familiar crush of people unloading, dragging, waiting for elevators, etc...We pulled right in front of the residence hall, a crew of students met us with a huge cart, helped us unload all within, then they asked us to park while they delivered the possessions to his room."

When they arrived at the room, "there were all his things just waiting for him to put away. [I]t was obvious that much planning had gone into making it as painless as possible. They even had cold drinks, snow cones and cotton candy. Thank you, CNU, for making our very first experience as a part of the entering class a very positive one. Perhaps other universities could take some lessons."[xii]

One of the most unusual—and time-consuming—ways that Paul Trible connected individually with potential students was through his admissions recruiting, particularly in the early days of CNU's transformation.

"When I came to Christopher Newport, a foreign student was someone from Fredericksburg," says Paul. "Most of our students lived a few miles from campus. We needed to attract young people from across Virginia, and truly become a state university. So Paul and others on the admissions team would brave the traffic on I-95 and head to northern Virginia, where the biggest concentration of high-ability students in the state happened to live. They would meet with guidance counselors individually or host them at group luncheons. They'd have open houses at night so students and their parents could come and hear the Christopher Newport story.

In Richmond, another academic hub, they established a yearly tradition at the iconic Jefferson Hotel. Every December Christopher Newport would host a festive luncheon for a hundred guidance counselors from the area, followed by an open house that evening for 400 potential students.

Such events pinned Christopher Newport on the minds of parents and guidance counselors, toward the goal of getting them to come to campus for tours, student panels, and presentations that highlighted the honors, leadership, and service programs. Professors and senior staff were available for discussion. Paul and Rosemary circulated as well.

"I dare say I'm the only president who is involved in admissions like this. I enjoy telling our story, which must be told with some power, precision, and persuasion. It also reflects one of our core values: the most important people on our campus are students. The fact that I meet thousands of prospective students reflects the importance

I place on students. If they are important, then by God, I should be actively involved in the admissions program. That's why Rosemary and I open our home to thousands of students, why I lead by wandering about, being visible and available on campus, having an open-door policy, so students know they can meet with me."

Once students arrive at Christopher Newport, the atmosphere is different from other schools. Of course, there is no dress code. Students, like students everywhere, come to class in their comfy clothes. But the idea of dressing in a way that is appropriate for various occasions is part of the culture. Clothing itself can be a courtesy, a way of honoring others and showing that they matter. One dresses up for a wedding or a funeral as a sign of celebration or respect. Make an appointment with an administration member at Christopher Newport, and he or she will be in a suit. A student once wrote,

"Yes, the grass is very green, and the buildings are very pretty. And it's the little things. All staff have their nametag on their right side so when they shake someone's hand the eye follows their arm up and reads their name...All this 'polish' rubs off on students, who you rarely see walking to class in sweatpants or pajamas even for their 8 a.m. classes. This is where the high bar CNU sets extends into other unintended details."

When Paul and Rosemary were on a trip to England years ago, they were reminded of the importance of occasional dress codes. Or perhaps, just the importance of dressing, period.

They were with friends at London's Ritz, an elegant, distinguished hotel, chatting with the concierge in the beautiful lobby area, which leads toward a richly appointed interior dining room and bar. Coats and ties were required for gentlemen who wished to dine and drink therein.

Suddenly there was a stir in the lobby. A businessman who just might have been imbibing a bit too much had lost a bet, stripped off all his clothes, and was sprinting out of the bar, heading for the lobby's glass doors. He did not realize they were locked. He got jammed up on the doors and couldn't get out, stuck like a naked bug on the glass, with his bum—as the British say—on display for all to see.

Rosemary Trible lifted her eyebrows at the concierge and nodded toward the doors. "Perhaps you'd better talk to that gentleman," she said. "He doesn't have a tie on."

Though you won't see many students with ties on at Christopher Newport unless it's a special occasion, students there do wear clothes. And little things make a difference.

Lacey Grey Hunter, who leads the President's Leadership Program, compares CNU's focus on "excellence in details" to the diamond system used to grade luxury hotel properties.

Some years ago, Lacey Grey worked at a premier resort that had lost its top-rated, four-diamond status. She saw the extraordinary lengths the resort undertook to regain its top billing, and the crucial importance of the little things. "Really, there's a very small difference in three-diamond versus four-diamond properties," Lacey Grey says today. They both have luxurious amenities and gorgeous settings. But the top-ranked properties pay more attention to every tiny detail. "We do that at Christopher Newport. We don't say 'no problem' when someone thanks us. That's negative. We say, 'my pleasure.' We don't abbreviate 'Virginia' or 'Street' or 'Avenue' on an envelope. We don't have tables at an event without tablecloths. We all pick up any piece of trash we might see on campus. We don't chew gum at events, and we don't talk to the people we already know—we look for guests we can welcome and get to know. We don't go on staff 'retreats.' We 'advance.'"

All this may sound a bit over the top, she realizes. But while in graduate school, Lacey Grey took classes at another fine Virginia university. She couldn't help but notice the overflowing trash cans everywhere. "It just generally felt to me like no one cared about the school," she says. "At Christopher Newport, we are establishing a brand, and we try to do so through excellence in all the details."

Every community is made up of people with all kinds of gifts, talents, and roles to play. The whole cannot function well unless every member is doing his or her part. Every person's particular role, whether he or she is a member of the faculty, administration, or support staff, is essential and important. People of different personalities, passions, backgrounds, belief systems, ethnicities, and histories are drawn together in a common sense of vocation or calling, something bigger than themselves.

Paul recently received a retirement letter that captures this reality.

"I am completing my career as a housekeeping professional with CNU. I say 'professional' with great gratitude and a sense of great pride. My career at CNU allowed me to flourish in more ways than can be imagined. I worked among a group of professionals from leadership to faculty and staff to the student population that made my days of employment joyful and full of excitement. I was eager every day to meet someone new and glean from their experiences. I was treated with kindness, love, and respect...I wish to thank you, President Trible, for setting the example of excellence that flowed down so that everyone could experience it and be encouraged to exemplify that same spirit. While I may not be with you every day, as I have for almost two decades, I will always be with you in spirit."

The importance of the individual in the community of kindness is also obvious in CNU's commitment to student success, starting with its emphasis on small classes. Large universities have all kinds of benefits, but first-year classes of several hundred people, taught by a graduate assistant are not one of them. It is so easy to get lost in the crowd.

At Christopher Newport, 65 percent of the classes are made up of 19 students or fewer. They are taught by full professors, not teaching assistants. At least one prof often brings students his wife's home-made muffins. He is quite popular. Professors know their students' names. Their office doors are always open. Students are not just a number, but each one is a valued individual in the group with a voice to be heard.

"Putting students first means that we listen, really listen, to their thoughts and concerns," Paul says. "It means that we are actively engaged in their lives. It means when we engage a student, we ask ourselves, 'what is the most loving, helpful, encouraging thing I can say or do right now? It means that Rosemary and I know hundreds of students by name. We know their hopes and dreams, and all too often, we know where their hearts are broken."

Dr. Lori Underwood also illustrates that "loving, helpful, encouraging" culture at Christopher Newport. She is Dean of the College of Arts and Humanities and directs CNU's Presidential Scholars Program. She is a dark-haired, diminutive woman with a soft-spoken yet steely way about her; her own life story has given her considerable compassion for students who are first-generation college students.

Lori was a bookish, curious, and precocious child whose mother taught her to read at age four so she would be healthily occupied and wouldn't get into something like mixing up chemicals and blowing up the house. The family lived in a rural area; Lori remembers going barefoot most of the time. "You only wore shoes if you were going to school, church, or the store, so you wouldn't wear them out." The family grew its own food; both money and the ability to imagine a wider life were tightly constrained.

Lori's academic gifts were discovered, however, and she eventually went to the University of Memphis on a full scholarship. She went on to get her master's degree there, and then her PhD in philosophy at the University of Missouri. She arrived at CNU as a professor in 1999, age 28, and became a dean in 2013.

"My own experience taught me the absolute transformative power of higher education," she says. "I have been able to take students around the world, to see great art, study in great libraries, and discuss classic ideas. My mom's idea of a vacation was to go camping a few miles from home. When I was young, we scrimped and saved; food options were limited. Now, if my children want something from the store, I tell them to just put it on the grocery list. And the things I do every day at work make the same type of transformation a possibility for my students."

Lori says that if any of her students are struggling, "there are five different offices I can call to connect them with help. Students know they can come to me. I can call any office on this campus. I know the people there, they know me, and, not in three to five days, but in three to five minutes, we can come up with a solution for any student."

Students appreciate Lori's care—and her teaching. In their own words:

"She's great. Beyond intelligent, but doesn't look down on students. She is helpful and has human understanding…If you do well—you earned it. Go see her a lot if you need to…it will help."

"Absolutely brilliant but kind, and she loves shoes. Her philosophy course on 'Radical Evil' is extremely creepy and intense in the best possible way."

"Best teacher on earth. She completely rocks. But she is tough. Fair but tough. Attendance isn't technically mandatory, but you won't survive if you don't show up. Her class is what education should be, full time, all the time. I love this woman!!!!"

For the past six years, Lori has created and run a global conference on opportunity and gender. She and her fellow leaders bring about 150 attendees from 120 different countries to Christopher Newport to discuss issues that many of these female scholars cannot safely talk about in their repressive societies at home—child marriage, violence, dowry killings, and sex trafficking. All such sessions are open to students.

Lori says that "one of the things I value most about CNU is that it is a place where female leadership is valued. It is truly a meritocracy, which is extremely unusual. People in higher ed are very good about *talking* about supporting women, but Christopher Newport is very good about *doing* something about it."

If you ask Lori how students have changed since she arrived at CNU in 1999, she'll tell you that there is measurable improvement in their capacity to capture sophisticated philosophical nuances. A specialist in Immanuel Kant, Lori says that she has colleagues in the same field in top universities across the country, and that she routinely teaches complex subject matter "that many of the fancy schools" reserve for grad students and "do not teach to undergraduates."

Lori's personal touch with students underscores how Christopher Newport's smaller size allows the school to care for its students by aligning its academic programs with students' particular learning needs and their potential for success.[xiii] Before their freshman year, students receive individualized course schedules to increase the likelihood of their first-term academic success. University fellows, recent graduates who serve as full-time "engagement advisors," contact all new students at least three times before school starts. They review, update, and change schedules as needed to fit with the students' particular propensities and educational goals.

After new students arrive on campus, they work with a faculty core advisor who will walk with them through their first two years as they pursue academic core requirements and major prerequisites. These advisors are required to meet with their students five times during the fall term. Significantly, only two of those sessions can focus on course selection and registration. The other meetings emphasize building relationships, engagement in academic support, educational planning, successfully transitioning to each next step, and co-curricular involvement.

Professors give academic feedback early on, by providing a "substantive grade" during the first four weeks of classes. This feedback means students and their advisors can make healthy changes in study habits or anything else as the semester rolls on.

There's also an "early-alert" system in which professors connect students with the Center for Academic Success, making students aware of the many resources available to them for academic help and encouragement.

Similarly, there's a Craigslist-type online program where students can post their academic needs and connect with peers who are looking to study together.

And finally, all first-year students participate in residential Living and Learning Communities; they live with the people taking the same general education courses, providing an organic support system.

One of the more colorful and convincing templates for student success takes place during freshmen orientation, when Provost David Doughty takes the stage. He minces no words, emphasizing over and over that the absolute key to doing well academically at Christopher Newport is to spend 25 hours a week studying and writing papers. This is, of course, on top of the 15 or so hours a week that most students carry as their course load.

How students get in those 25 hours a week is entirely up to them, says Dave. But they must have a plan. He helpfully suggests several options.

First, there is the plain vanilla 9–5 Plan. Students perceive Monday to Friday as a 40-hour work week and combine their classes and their personal study into five eight-hour-a day work blocks.

This tends to work very well, says Dave.

Then there is the Frisbee Plan. In this happy strategy, students go to their classes each day and spent the balance of their daytime hours tossing frisbees on the Great Lawn or sipping coffee with their friends. Then from 7 p.m. to midnight each evening, they study. Hard.

This, too, can work well.

Third, we have the Trash Your Weekends Plan. You go to class and otherwise relax during the week, and then study for 13 hours on Saturday and 12 hours on Sunday.

People who do this have no weekend social life, but this plan is still feasible, at least in theory.

Finally, says Dave, there is the Failure Plan. And that, of course, is having no plan.

Dr. Lisa Duncan Raines is Vice President of Enrollment and Student Success. She oversees networks of offices across Christopher Newport's campus that help students with academics, career planning, financial aid, and all kinds of other support services. If you sit down and talk with Lisa, you see that she's a gifted administrator—her PhD is in higher education leadership—and that she has a heart full of compassion and empathy for students and their challenges.

One of the basic student success tools that Lisa and her colleagues use is the College Student Inventory, a survey used by 1400 universities across the U.S. that helps colleges identify students who might be at academic risk in particular areas, creating support intervention that can turn the tide before new students get bogged down in patterns of failure.

Lisa smiles as she remembers students that Christopher Newport was able to help along the way. One "really tall, burly guy" a few years ago desperately wanted to major in math, but he just could not succeed in one of the essential upper-level courses.

Lisa met with him. "We need a Plan B," she told him. They talked for hours. "I'll NEVER graduate," he moaned. She suggested an economics major as an alternative; it would use his affinities for math but would focus his energies on another discipline. He started taking economics courses. He loved them. When Lisa would see him at his on-campus job, he walked a little taller. "Then he graduated," Lisa says. "He just got married and is starting a new job. I'm so proud of him!"

Sometimes students come to college, and it becomes clear that their parents have expectations that they will follow a certain course of study and a certain career track that just doesn't fit with the students' particular gifts and skills. One student who had come from a small, private school in northern Virginia was fixated on going to CNU's Luter School of Business. But he really struggled academically. The Center for Academic Success worked with him and helped him realize that a business major was just not his thing. He switched to communications, and halfway through his second year, he really hit his stride. "So many people told me he would not graduate," Lisa says. "I was really worried about him. I always kept my eye on him. I knew how hard he was working, and I could not have been prouder."

Lisa worked in the student success offices at Virginia Tech for 17 years before she came to Christopher Newport in 2003 for a job interview. She knew nothing about Christopher Newport except that it was small and had a ship's wheel on its transcript, but "I fell in love with the community here." So she stayed.

What has she appreciated about Paul Trible?

"To have a leader that doesn't just talk servant leadership, but actually lives it, is refreshing and inspiring. CNU really is a magical place. When people say, 'oh, it's just a shiny bubble,' I always say, 'come and feel what it's like here.' It's love. A culture of *kindness*. I don't think the Tribles could work the hours they work—and only one of them is on the payroll—without deeply loving the students and this place."

Kevin Hughes came to work at Christopher Newport in 2000, while he was a doctoral student at William & Mary in educational policy planning and leadership. Today he serves as Vice President of Student Affairs and Dean of Students. His job, like that of everyone else one talks to at Christopher Newport, is enormous, full of challenges, and fun. "What I've loved since I came here is that we've had the opportunity to build and create things from the ground up." CNU, as a young school, has been fertile ground for building traditions, programs, and culture.

For example, when Kevin first came to campus, there were perhaps three national sororities and four fraternities, one of which had four members. Christopher Newport's leadership wanted to build up a robust Greek system, bringing energy to the entire campus. Now there are over 1200 students in Greek life.

The intention has always been that these Greek students not just participate in their fraternity or sorority, but also be involved in the leadership program, on athletic teams, tutoring in the public schools, helping local special Olympics...at Christopher Newport, the emphasis is on cross-pollination, whatever one's passions. Yes, pursue your interests, develop your friend groups, but don't lock down in separate silos. Mix with everyone else on campus as much as you can. The result will make campus culture stronger and more diverse.

Kevin, like every other senior administrator or faculty member at CNU, has not allowed his executive position to diminish his contact with students. Though he oversees everything from residential advisors to student activities to counseling and health services to equipping students to embrace Christopher Newport's honor system, he still reaches out to help individual people.

"I believe in character development. Our honor system, for example, is not just about rules, don't lie, cheat, or steal. It's about becoming an honorable person. It's about character. That is part of what student affairs is about. I love how we go out of our way to find solutions for students, whatever it is they are dealing with. Some say we hold hands too much. No, it's called guiding people. That's our obligation. I feel like parents have entrusted their most precious gift to us; we have the responsibility in stewardship of that trust."

Sometimes Kevin gets calls at night at home from parents or students who are facing tough issues. One night his kids asked him, "Dad, why are you on the phone with them during your time off?"

"Because," Kevin responded, "that's what I would want someone to do for you if you were in need."

CHAPTER 12

SAILING IN THE SAME BOAT

"If you want to go quickly, go alone.
If you want to go far, go together."

— *AFRICAN PROVERB*

I f people matter at Christopher Newport, then inclusion, diversity, justice, and mercy are vital to cultivating its culture of kindness. During the tragic, chaotic, and searing summer of 2020, communities across the nation seethed with pain and outrage after the brutal murder on May 25 of George Floyd, a 46-year-old Black resident of Minneapolis, by Derek Chauvin, a 44-year-old White police officer. (Chauvin would later be found guilty of all charges.)

In June 2020, a few days after George Floyd's death, CNU Rector Bobby Hatten gave a long, impassioned statement before a public meeting of the Board of Visitors. His remarks are worth quoting at length.

"I would like to take a moment of personal privilege to speak to everyone in the Commonwealth of Virginia who is listening," Bobby began.

"We have a crisis of structural and intractable racism in America. It is obvious and blatant to everyone who has eyes to see and a heart to understand. So obvious that the entire country has just seen a police officer murder a Black man in broad daylight, slowly killing him with his knee on his neck, while three other officers stood by and did nothing to stop it. That crime, as well as other atrocities by police, has ignited the justifiable rage and anger of millions of Americans—Black, Brown and White—who are still marching through our cities and towns..."

"One thing is certain: White people, like me, DO NOT KNOW what it is like to be Black in America, But IF this week has taught us anything, it has taught us that it is time—long past time—that White men and women in America need to start listening to Black people and standing up with them..."

"Enough is enough. White people can no longer look away and refuse to confront these issues. It is long past time for broad-reaching changes to our laws and our culture to root out and destroy racism against Black and Brown people in America.

"As leaders of this great university, we have heard the voices of the Black community and we support you. Your voices, thoughts, and feelings matter to the university, but we want you to know that we have not been waiting for this national tragedy to respond."

Bobby went on to detail what Christopher Newport had already been doing, saluting his old friend in the process.

"Under the progressive leadership of President Paul Trible, last year we instituted the Community Captains program to directly change the lives of economically disadvantaged children in Newport News, most of whom are Black...This progressive program is unmatched by any other college or university in the state of Virginia.

"Last week the University Council on Diversity and Inclusion, led by our colleagues Sheriff Gabe Morgan and Brad Hunter, and including students, faculty, staff, alumni, and leaders from the community—submitted Christopher Newport's Strategic Plan for Diversity, Equity, and Inclusion to the Commonwealth of Virginia.

"This 25-page document outlines a bold plan of action for the University to overcome the remaining burdens of historical racism in higher education...

"I am pleased to report that our focus on attracting more students of color has increased the number of Black students we expect to welcome to our freshman class based on deposits received, 91 Black students versus 78 last year—an increase of 16 percent. The Community Captains Program that I have just described will swell those numbers of Black students in future years.

"Paul Trible's mantra and CNU's mission is to change hearts and minds so that we can provide leadership to our community, our state, and our country..." Quoting the old Bill Withers song, "Lean on Me," Bobby concluded, "CNU's message to our students and to this community is simple: Lean on us because Black lives do matter at CNU, and we intend to play a leadership role in changing the hearts and minds of our students, our community, and our country so that we can end the crisis of racism that is so destructive to our national ideals of equality, fairness, and justice."

The Community Captains program to which Bobby referred had hatched years earlier in the fertile, mustachioed mind of Provost David Doughty back in 2014. Christopher Newport had relationships with medical schools where CNU pre-med students who qualified could be provisionally admitted.

"Why not do the same type of thing at Christopher Newport," Dave thought, "with high school students who come from low-income areas in our city?"

After a few years of behind-the-scenes work, Christopher Newport officially unveiled Community Captains, an early admission, two-year college preparatory program that helps minority students of limited financial means to succeed after high school. It is open to sophomores at Newport News public high schools who have a grade point of 3.4 or an 1150 score out of 1600 on their PSAT, who would be first-generation college students, or who attest significant financial need.

Those who qualify receive two years of free, on-campus and virtual learning opportunities at Christopher Newport, as well as a free class for college credit. Students are also carefully paired with CNU student mentors. "This program offers myriad advantages to our students," Newport News Public Schools superintendent George Parker told the press, "including ongoing mentorship by CNU volunteers, additional college and career advisement and the ability to experience a class at CNU as a high school senior."[xiv]

The first Community Captains arrived on campus as first-year students, full of high hopes and great expectations, in fall 2021.

"It's a cool initiative," says Provost Doughty. "It could potentially be scaled up to include other local communities."

In July 2020, Paul Trible issued a statement reflecting on the challenging and painful opportunities he had had to dialogue, learn, and mourn over the pain that summer of 2020 had brought to so many lives. "I have had the opportunity to communicate with hundreds of students, faculty, staff and alumni, meet virtually with the Executive Committee of the Multicultural Alumni Chapter, march with hundreds on our campus and read and reflect. I believe this can be a defining moment for our campus and country and we must all work to create a freer and fairer America."

At George Floyd's memorial service in early June 2020, North Central University President Scott Hagan challenged every college to establish an undergraduate scholarship to contribute toward the educational promise of aspiring young Black Americans. CNU accordingly launched the Inclusive Excellence Scholarship, with an initial leadership gift from Distinguished Professor Dr. Lisa Spiller. This joined other CNU funds already in place to recruit and assist minority students, like the Alumni Achievement Endowment and the Create a Captain Annual Scholarship, whose primary purpose is to help those students for whom Christopher Newport is their dream school, but that dream is out of reach because of financial hardship.

During that summer of 2020, Paul also announced the appointment of Angela Spranger as Assistant to the President for Equity and Engagement and Christopher Newport's Chief Diversity, Equity and Inclusion Officer.

Angela Spranger is a tall, regal woman with energy brimming inside of her, as if she knows a secret. Back in 1988, when she was a senior in high school in Highland Springs, Virginia, she was selected to be part of a group of young leaders from across the nation to come to Washington, D.C. for a five-day leadership program and participate in a mock congress. (Angela was the Democratic party whip.) They toured the Capitol, other D.C. sites, and the Virginia delegation visited with one of their United States senators, Paul Trible, in his office. Angela still has the group photo taken that day. Both she and Paul look rather different today.

It would be 24 years until Paul and Angela's paths converged again. Angela went on to get her BA in psychology, then her MBA, a Master's in Education in Human and Organizational Learning, and her PhD in organizational leadership.

This woman *loves* school.

She worked for years in the human resources arena at Newport News Shipbuilding, then arrived at Christopher Newport in 2012 as an instructor, and then a lecturer in management in the Luter School of Business until she won conversion to the tenure track in 2019. Then Paul tapped her for her new role. Her initial priorities, Paul announced, would include:

- implementing the Strategic Plan for Diversity and Inclusion that had been recently approved by the Council on Diversity and Inclusion;
- creating community conversations about the Black experience, racism and injustice in housing, education, health care, jobs and other institutions;
- planning and implementing a training program on racism, diversity, inclusion, and equity that will be required for all students, faculty and staff;

- working with the provost, deans and faculty to develop curricular and co-curricular opportunities for CNU's students to understand racial inequity and how to create change as they lead, serve and engage in our society;
- working to recruit, engage and retain faculty, staff and students of color at Christopher Newport;
- facilitating regular dialogues about policing and individual rights;
- revamping Christopher Newport's programming to celebrate the life and legacy of Dr. Martin Luther King, Jr.

Angela says that this rather ambitious seven-point plan requires her to embrace her inner Black Super Woman, a role she says is not unfamiliar to women of any color. But she has felt buoyed and energized by a tide of enthusiasm from her CNU community: "this position did not come out of nowhere. I felt like I was at the front of a juggernaut of energy. Everyone was ready for these kinds of conversations."

Part of that energy came from Brad Hunter, a member of Christopher Newport's Board of Visitors and Vice Rector of the university. He's a soft-spoken and agreeable guy who graduated with a degree in accounting from CNU's President's Leadership Program in 2004. He was drawn both to CNU's in-state cost and that leadership program, as he had done a lot of volunteer work, leadership, and service in his community and church while in high school. "CNU added so much context to what had already been inherently instilled in me by my parents," says Brad. "I saw how organizations can be impacted by good leadership."

As a student, Brad served as president of Christopher Newport's multicultural students association, and, among other things, as a student director responsible for training upper-class orientation leaders.

Through Paul Trible's help, Brad interned with Witt Mares & Co. while he was an undergraduate, and the company hired him as a staff accountant after his graduation. He went on to get his MBA at

Syracuse University. Today he serves as a commercial banking officer and a vice president of TowneBank.

A few years ago, Brad led an alumni push to create a new Alumni Achievement Endowment to support academically distinguished students who have overcome unusual adversity, as well as those from underrepresented groups that enrich Christopher Newport's campus diversity.

"Once I got on the Alumni Society Board and started talking with other graduates, one of the things that resonated with us was the experience we had being a part of the Multicultural Student Association," he says. "It had a big impression on us and our college careers. Many of us are still friends and connected even though we're spread out across the country."

Funding such an endowment would require $50,000. Former Christopher Newport rector Preston White got excited about the idea and told the alumni that if they could raise $25,000 by a certain deadline, he'd match it, dollar for dollar.

They did. And he did.

"It was the brainchild of a large group of alumni," Brad says. "We wanted to give back in whatever small way we could so other minority students could have the same great experience we had at CNU."

Creating a place that is diverse, inclusive, and unified is a delicate process. It requires a community of character, where people value one another, speak to one another, and are willing to listen, truly listen to one another.

This is not only true in terms of racial identity, but in matters of gender identity. Christopher Newport's Vice Provost Dr. Geoffrey Klein started the LGBTQ+ and Allies Faculty/Staff Affinity Group. As a gay man in a leadership role on campus, Geoffrey said he recognized the need for more voices to serve as a resource for all students on campus.

"I think this group helps to contribute to the sense that diversity isn't just one thing, that we can think about diversity of thought, diversity of individuals, orientations or skin color," Geoffrey says.

"It's nice to be able to have these types of opportunities for these communities to get together and have conversations that help move the campus community forward in the wide efforts for enhancing inclusion and diversity."

Paul Trible says, "We must believe that everyone who crosses our path...has something important to impart. If we are willing to listen—really listen—and learn from others, then great things are possible. This is why the pursuit of diversity and inclusion on our campus and in our world is so important. This is the genius of America, a rich mosaic of different colors and hues, different religions, philosophies, and politics. We must learn to engage each other, learn from each other and work with each other."

Angela Spranger notes that, "One thing I've learned is that you'd better not assume that just because your words feel right to you doesn't mean that they will be understood by someone else. What that means is that we all must approach one another with *humility*. And that means truly becoming allies."

"Allies" is a buzz word in cultural arenas these days. To Angela, what that can mean—whether in supporting someone of a different race than oneself or of a different sexual orientation—is best illustrated by a personal story.

One summer day when racial tensions simmered across the country, Angela and her husband were driving in an urban area when they were pulled over by a police officer. Angela, who was driving, is Black. Her husband, Keith, is White.

Based on lifelong experience, as well as the unrest of those summer days, Angela carefully kept both hands on the steering wheel as the officer approached the car. Her heart raced and she was breathing fast. She couldn't help it.

"Officer, the vehicle registration is in the glove compartment," she said to the police officer. "And my driver's license is in the bag that is resting on the back seat behind me." She kept her hands right on the wheel.

"Oh!" said her husband. "I wondered where it was. No worries! I'll just grab it."

He twisted and leaned toward the back seat to get Angela's purse.

"Nooooo!" breathed Angela. What was he doing? No Black person would unthinkingly make such a sudden move; the officer might assume he or she was going for a gun.

Keith turned back around, the purse in his hands. "I've got it."

The officer looked at the documents, went back to his cruiser and checked them out, then returned and told Angela that her tags were expired. "Get them updated at the DMV, and have a good day," he concluded.

Afterwards, Angela couldn't stop shaking. "You don't understand," she said to her husband. "Black people and White people have a totally different experience and expectation when they are dealing with the police."

"Well," said Keith, "You can share my privilege any time."

They laughed, and then Angela drove—very carefully—toward their destination. To Angela, Keith's words capture what it means to be an ally with someone who is part of any minority group. Let me listen to you. Let me share my privilege with you. Let me get into your situation with you, so we're sailing in the same boat.

CHAPTER 13

A COMMUNITY
OF HONOR

"You will never do anything in this world without courage. It is the greatest quality of the mind next to honor."

— *ARISTOTLE*

C hristopher Newport is by no means perfect, but the university
intentionally strives to continue to build its culture of kindness.
Foundational to that culture is attentiveness to the university years
as a time to grow in strength of character, to become a person of
integrity, discernment, and honor.

Several of the most important traditions that underscore these
core values happen each August. As first-year students unpack at
Christopher Newport before classes start, they do the things freshmen
across America do when they arrive at college. They make multiple
trips to Target, madly buying cleaning supplies, toilet bowl brushes,
sheets, towels, hanging lights, curtains, sponges, and dish soap. Some
of these items are purchased at the insistence of their parents, and
will never be used. Friendships form; there are frisbee games on the
lawn, many cups of coffee consumed, social anxiety, and all the questions and possibilities that come with new beginnings.

During this time, Christopher Newport puts a great deal of emphasis on its honors convocation, which takes place the week before upper class students arrive and classes start. Freshmen wear business attire and take their seats in the Ferguson Center's Diamonstein Concert Hall. On stage, members of the Christopher Newport brass ensemble play chamber music for horn, trumpet, trombone, and tuba. The nearly 300 members of the faculty file in in solemn array, led by the most senior faculty member, Dr. Jay Paul, who directs the university's academic honors program. He carries the four-foot-long university mace. Each professor is attired in his or her academic robes, ceremonial hats, and other regalia; the stage is a swirl of rich fabrics, reds, blues, burgundies, tassels, and gold and silver insignia. It is a grand occasion, weighted with gravitas, the type of ritual one encounters less and less in today's casual culture.

If students have the ears to hear, the speeches affirm that they are at an important crossroads, that they are becoming part of a community of honor and learning, with all the rights and privileges that entails. They are reminded that Dr. Martin Luther King, Jr. wrote, when he was an 18-year-old college student, that "intelligence plus character—that is the goal of true education." They are directed to think about honesty, integrity, dedication, generosity, and compassion, that these are elements of character that can be practiced and developed during their time at CNU. They hear other students affirm that "It's not easy to live this way, but it is the right way to live."

The members of the entire assembly stand together. They recite the honor code, and the first-year students come forward to sign a registry that indicates their solemn pledge:

> "On my honor, I will maintain the highest standards of honesty, integrity and personal responsibility. This means I will not lie, cheat or steal, and as a member of this academic community, I am committed to creating an environment of respect and mutual trust."

Told that their success will certainly depend on hard work and a little luck, each student is given a "lucky penny," which the more organized among them will keep during their four years in college, and then toss into CNU's campus fountain on their graduation day. The penny comes with a dedication written by a much-loved English professor and associate provost who passed away several years ago, Dr. Tracey Schwarze:

> *To give your word and keep it as a person of integrity;*
> *To treasure the life of the mind and the spirit of*
> *intellectual inquiry;*
> *To value richness of character over richness of purse;*
> *To give, because to you, much has been given;*
> *To seek important work — and to do it with all your*
> *heart.*
> *Keep this faith as you become a citizen of CNU, of the*
> *nation*
> *and the world*
> *And one day*
> *As you remember*
> *The grandeur of the Ferguson Center,*
> *The beauty of the Great Lawn,*
> *The tranquility of the James, and*
> *The friends and mentors of your youth.*
> *You will know that you have lived a life of honor and*
> *significance ...*

Paul Trible always ends his own speech on this day of solemn pledges with a story from when his son and namesake was young.

When Paul III was a senior in college, his 22-year-old friend, Cullum Owings, was killed by a speeding tractor-trailer as he and his brother returned to college on the Sunday after Thanksgiving break. Though his brother was not severely injured, Cullum died at the scene.

Cullum's dad told CBS News, "That morning when we went to church, he talked to me about the application for the Peace Corps, and he said, 'Dad, you know a lot of people apply for this because they know it will look good on their resume. I want to get in because I want to do the work.'"[xv]

At Cullum's memorial service, Paul III and others wept as passages were read from his journal. These were written during his first year of college; he had no idea, of course, that they would be read at his funeral just four years later.

"I truly realize now what is important for the rest of my life. I want to be well educated in life. I want a group of friends whom I enjoy spending time with and who love me. I want to marry a woman I know I'm in love with. I want to make a decent living, but live below my means. I want to find God and spend lots of time contemplating him and conversing with him.

"I want to grow old with the woman I love, spend time with grandkids, cry at funerals and weddings, and die a happy, successful, respected, loved, and content man."

After these paragraphs, Cullum had written:

"Look at this every year. *Become this man. Lead this life.*"

"College is the time for each of you to choose what kind of man or woman you will become and what kind of life you will lead," President Trible tells the honors convocation students. "So choose wisely. The pursuit of power, position, wealth, fame, fun? None of these things matter at the end of your days. We were put on earth to make a contribution, to make a difference, to live a life of significance. Keep your ending in mind...even at the beginning."

CHAPTER 14

SERVING THE WORLD, ONE PERSON AT A TIME

"I alone cannot change the world, but I can cast
a stone across the waters to create many ripples."

— *MOTHER TERESA*

"I think my role in creating social change is building an envi-
roment of mutual respect and tolerance across cultural, lin-
guistic, and religious differences...to promote cross-cultural
learning and experiences as a blessing rather than a burden,
so that peace may spread like wildfire in our community."

— *CNU GRADUATE EMMA SEGUIN*

A s we'll see in the next chapter, Christopher Newport people like
to say that getting an education there depends on four pillars of
"co-curricular engagement that amplifies students' academic accomplishments." Those mainstays are undergraduate research, internships,
study abroad, and service.

Service is a distinctive on that list, for it is not only something
that one does, like engaging in research or studying abroad, but is a
part of who one *is*. Being a person who serves others is a life attribute
that endures after academic research or travel has come to an end. It
can be lived out in any context, in any season, for the rest of one's life.

Christopher Newport provides a rich array of opportunities for students. They can learn how to effectively serve others, discover what arenas of service they are drawn toward and are good at, and enjoy the unique satisfaction of blessing others during one's college years, a season that can otherwise sometimes slide into a rather self-oriented lifestyle.

Today's world at large, and any particular community, are full of needs, brimming with people who can use physical or emotional help, resources, and love. The needs can become overwhelming.

Decades ago, Rosemary Trible traveled to Calcutta, India. She spent a week at Nirmal Hriday, the hospice Mother Teresa founded in 1952 for the sick, destitute, and dying poor. It received worldwide attention, particularly after Mother Teresa received the Nobel Peace Prize in 1979. Rosemary worked among the poorest of the poor, caring for those who were dying. She also had the extraordinary opportunity to talk with Mother Teresa, who would pass away in 1997.

Every day, the nuns and volunteers would go out to the byways of the city. They would find dying beggars, abandoned children, the human "trash" discarded on Calcutta's teeming streets. They tenderly picked up those who were riddled with disease, terrified because of mental illness, or unable to care for themselves. They brought them back to the home, washed them, cared for them, sang to them, and prayed for them. They held the hands of the dying. After all, as Mother Teresa (now Saint Teresa) had said, "a beautiful death is for people who lived like animals to die like angels—loved and wanted."

Like every visitor who volunteers at this place, Rosemary felt overwhelmed by the relentless tide of death, despair, decay, and disease. She knew that the Missionaries of Charity believed that God had called them to a life of faithfulness in the face of enormous need, a calling that was not distracted by western notions of "success."

As it drew near time for Rosemary to return to the United States, she told Mother Teresa about her feelings of powerlessness, given the immensity of the need. "How do you do this in the midst of so much despair and poverty?" she asked the world-renowned leader, who stood just under five feet tall, and was now confined to a wheelchair.

"Ah, Rosemary," said Mother Teresa, "We are not called to be successful. We are called to be faithful."

"What can I do to really make a difference?" Rosemary asked.

Mother Teresa smiled, her face a holy roadmap of wrinkles. She had a way of cutting to the chase. "Go home, Rosemary, and do whatever is in front of you," she told Rosemary, lifting her hands in a blessing. "You start by loving the person right in front of you."

Paul Trible often tells that story in speeches to Christopher Newport students. "Changing the world" and "setting the world on fire" can be grand and inspiring rhetoric, but what does changing the world, one person at a time, really look like?

From the beginning of Paul's tenure at Christopher Newport, he was determined that the university would be a place where students could find answers to that question. Christopher Newport not only provides an atmosphere where service is an assumed civic virtue, but the university also provides dozens of practical opportunities that pull students into helping real people in the Newport News communities around CNU's beautiful campus.

Even before classes start each year, CNU borrows a fleet of Newport News public school buses, divides up and loads 1000 new students into them, and sends groups of students out to waiting community nonprofits all over the city. The students clean up and decorate public schools for the new academic year. They paint and refurbish old buildings that have fallen into disrepair. They pick up trash. They pack food distribution kits and shiny new backpacks full of school supplies. They smile at everyone, talk with residents, and play with small children.

For many of the Christopher Newport students, it's a first glimpse, up close, of previously unmet needs. It's the first time they hear stories from people who have not had advantages the students might take for granted. It's the first time they can see how hands-on helping can really make a difference. Small, yes, but CNU's annual Day of Service can be a beginning of a lifestyle of *many* days of service.

For a student named Emma Seguin, Christopher Newport's focus on civic service meant helping refugee families settle in a new land with help and hope.

Emma is a red-headed, freckled young woman with a quick smile and a willingness to connect with people wherever they are. She's also the kind of person who will eat a live African termite, including wings, on a dare. You probably don't want to mess with Emma.

Emma graduated from Christopher Newport in 2021. While still in high school, she had gone on service trips to the Democratic Republic of the Congo and discovered she had an organic love for serving overseas. When she arrived at CNU in the fall of 2017, Emma started working with a refugee resettlement, teaching English as a Second Language classes, and building relationships with Congolese families who had fled violence in their homeland and were trying to establish a new life in Newport News. She helped them learn self-sufficiency skills, like planting gardens so they could sell produce at local farmers' markets.

Then, to her enormous shock and delight, she met a new family that had settled in the Newport News area—but they were not new to her. She had already gotten to know them during her trips to serve in the Congo.

Emma majored in Spanish, with minors in Human Rights and Conflict Resolution and Leadership Studies. She worked as a barista at Einstein's and participated in a four-year scholarship program in partnership with the national Bonner Foundation. These Bonner Scholars follow a four-year developmental pathway. First, they explore the history and culture of Newport News, along with 10 service tracks that include areas like youth development, hunger and housing, and arts and culture. The students then connect with one of those areas they have a passion for and become regular volunteers at one of the Center's vetted community partners. Third-and fourth-year students often pair their continued service work with community-based undergraduate research, international service, or senior-level capstone projects that benefit their service site.

"Through the Bonner program," says Emma Seguin, "I was able to develop skills necessary for building cross-cultural relationships, gain practice teaching, and deepen my global perspective." Her advice for new Christopher Newport students is to find a service site they love and "dive in head-first. Become friends with the people you serve, and live life alongside them—even when life gets hard."

Asked for one of the quotes that inspires her, Emma cites Dr. Martin Luther King, Jr.'s writings about the biblical parable of the Good Samaritan.

"I imagine that the first question the priest and Levite asked was: 'If I stop to help this man, what will happen to me?'

"But by the very nature of his concern, the good Samaritan reversed the question: 'If I do not stop to help this man, what will happen to *him*?'"

Most Christopher Newport students pursue service aside from the Bonner scholarship. All undergraduates are encouraged to enroll in the Service Distinction Program; every student who completes 100 hours of community service receives this graduation honor. Those interested in the scholarship of civic and community engagement can participate in the Service Distinction Leader Program and get a minor in civic engagement and social justice.

Jessie Deal graduated from Christopher Newport with a degree in environmental biology in 2015, and followed up with a masters in environmental sciences. She started working with CNU's Community Engagement Director Vanessa Buehlman in 2018. She was excited to help students in the same way the center had helped her.

"When I was a freshman, I had a difficult time connecting with my new community of Newport News," she says. "But the Center for Community Engagement helped me identify organizations that served the Newport News community and helped get me connected." As she gained confidence, Jessie discovered that she *loved* going into local neighborhoods in Newport News and building relationships with the residents.

"I learned what their stories are, their dreams, and their struggles," she says. Once she identified with the people, it was easy to love and serve their community. "And when you serve in the same area over your four years of college, you develop strong relationships there over time. So now I try to equip students to enter neighborhoods in a healthy way, to understand themselves—the lens they see through—and to understand how to interact well with the residents."

Jessie and Vanessa's enthusiasm for their work at Christopher Newport's Center for Community Engagement is infectious. Talk with them together, and they'll finish each other's sentences, and almost interrupt each other with examples of students' initiative and faithfulness in helping people in need.

Raising awareness of the under-served communities surrounding Christopher Newport begins even before first-year students move onto campus. During orientation, they're introduced to a sort of "Newport News 101" that gives the histories of various communities that are part of the city.

Take, for example, the Marshall Ridley community, located adjacent to the Hampton Roads harbor and I-664, a neighborhood with a rich African American heritage. Historically home to many Black shipyard workers and administrators, it was once a thriving middle class residential area that grew with the shipbuilding and military economic boom in the first half of the 20th century, but later fell into decline.

Several years ago, Marshall Ridley received a grant from the Department of Housing and Urban Development to rebuild distressed public housing, improve services, expand learning opportunities, create pathways to jobs, and strengthen families. All kinds of community action programs came alongside—groups like Habitat for Humanity, The Boys & Girls Club, Newport News Shipbuilding, the United Way, the Downtown Newport News Merchants & Neighbors Association, and Christopher Newport University, to name just a few.

If the ongoing work in the Marshall Ridley neighborhood represents working alongside established nonprofits, some of Christopher Newport's service ideas have come directly from students. Take, for example, the Food Fighters, which grew out of several students' abashed realization of just how much uneaten, good food was getting wasted at CNU's dining halls.

They organized themselves and recruited others to help. Now student volunteers collaborate with the dining staff to create a community effort against waste. Each evening, dining staffers package leftover food in containers provided by the Food Co-op, a local food pantry. Students deliver the food—which include quality proteins and healthy fruits and vegetables that are expensive for charities to obtain otherwise—to local distribution points on Monday through Friday of every full academic week.

A few months after the program began, one such group, the Peninsula Rescue Mission, reported that their monthly food costs had declined by 30 percent, freeing resources for other needs.

A few years ago, a biology major named Kayla Kamper and her roommate, Katy Ingalls, started a service group called Innovative Minds. It's a student service organization that brings STEM learning to Boys and Girls Clubs near Christopher Newport's campus. "I've always valued serving others," Kayla says, "but it was not until I became a Captain that I experienced the true impact service can have on a person."

Innovative Minds introduces children to basic scientific principles through fun, interactive experiments, like baking soda volcanoes, exploding lemons, and building ramps for toy cars to show real-world physics concepts. "We wanted to help these kids learn to love science and education," Kayla says. "One little girl told me she wanted to be a scientist so she could help her sister, who has diabetes. She asked me questions about college and said she wanted to study science like me." Kayla has since graduated from CNU, but current Christopher Newport students continue on in the great program she started.

Christopher Newport students also work with volunteers from All Nations Church, which opens its doors every Sunday to the homeless in Newport News. A bus travels to pick up people in need and bring them to a center where they dine on eggs, bacon, fruit, and all the trimmings. They also receive a large bag of food from the pantry, medical care, clothing and a shower. Most important, they feel like human beings, cared for and valued by the volunteers who welcome them.

Kesem is a nationwide community, driven by passionate college student leaders, which comes alongside little children who are experiencing the confusion, fear, and anxiety of a parent's cancer. Students engage with kids in fun programs that open the door to ongoing relationships that can comfort and strengthen the children both during and after their mom or dad's cancer journey.

Best Buddies offers other opportunities for students to serve. It's a nationwide program that helps people who have intellectual and developmental disabilities like Down syndrome, autism, Williams syndrome, cerebral palsy, and other undiagnosed health challenges. Or students can work with Natasha House, helping moms and children who are working their way out of homelessness even as they deal with the aftermath of abuse. They can mentor students in STEM subjects at Crittenden Middle School. Or they can work with Special Olympics, the United Way, the Virginia Living Museum, or dozens of other avenues for service.

It is officially unknown how many Dolly Parton fans can be found among college students, but Yorktown native Kyle DeGood was one of them.

Kyle graduated from Christopher Newport in 2020. As a student at the Luter School of Business, he was mentored by management professor Dr. Willy Donaldson, and got excited about channeling his growing business acumen toward efforts that do good for others. He pursued Christopher Newport's minor in civic engagement and social entrepreneurship, an interdisciplinary blend of study and service. He launched his own nonprofit venture, the DeGood Foundation, which develops programs for youth health education and literacy.

Because of Kyle's affinity for Dolly, he was aware of the country music superstar's Imagination Library, a global child literacy endeavor that Dolly Parton founded in 1996. It's a program that sends kids a free book every month from the time they're born until they start kindergarten. The books are specifically curated to match critical developmental stages, and cover themes like love, kindness, shapes, colors, numbers, and animals.

Kyle had seen the simple power of the written word when he would read out loud to his young sisters. "Reading is the ultimate foundation for education," he says. "And for newborns up to age five, it's when the most neurological connections are made in the brain."

Kyle started his DeGood Foundation to develop programs for youth health in education and literacy while he was still a student. The Foundation launched a local Imagination Library, and Kyle's business savvy equipped him to find corporate sponsors as well as likeminded local partners. He developed an additional program, Bags of Hope, which brings warmth, love, and fun to children facing extended stays in the hospital. Kyle partners in this with the Children's Hospital of the King's Daughters, a Tidewater, Virginia medical center that Kyle credits with saving his own life at birth. Volunteers stock the bags with simple items that convey a lot of love: a squishy, custom-stuffed bear for warm hugs at scary moments; a custom coloring book, activity and reading books, crayons, toy cars, and a signed card from the volunteer who packed the bag.

Reflecting on Kyle's charitable entrepreneurship, Vanessa Buehlman says, "These kids blow me away constantly. Now CNU students volunteer with Kyle's foundation. It just shows what one person can do."

Vanessa's co-conspirator Jessie Deal adds, "We're constantly reaching out into new areas, learning about communities. At the end of every year when we look back—in the midst of all the craziness in the world—these students give us so much hope. It sounds so sappy, but it's true. The fact that these students are going out to serve the world gives us hope."

CHAPTER 15

PILLARS

"Truth is the faith of academic life. Honor is the ethical compass which guides us all in the practice of this faith. Together, they make learning valuable, teaching credible, and wisdom possible. These are precious gifts."

—*DR. RICHARD SUMMERVILLE,*
FORMER CNU PROVOST

C olumns abound at Christopher Newport University. This is clear if you walk around the manicured campus. The majestic scale of the stately Georgian buildings built during the last 25 years draws the eye upward; soaring, white columns evoke a sense of classical beauty, symmetry, and permanence. This place is solid.

So, it is no surprise that Christopher Newport's academic programs rest on four co-curricular *pillars*—service, as we have already seen, as well as undergraduate research, internships, and study abroad. While profiling these areas of endeavor, one is tempted to detail every single opportunity and program, but a faithful replication of Christopher Newport's undergraduate catalogue, and its supporting documents, would not be particularly helpful here. You can check those out online.

UNDERGRADUATE RESEARCH

CNU's smaller size, and attention to relationships between faculty and students, means students don't need to wait until graduate school to pursue academic research. Christopher Newport emphasizes this because, as Provost Doughty often says, succeeding in the world beyond college (sometimes known as the "real world," although that is debatable) depends far more on research skills than it does on one's competence in a classroom setting.

Christopher Newport professors, in a variety of different disciplines, open opportunities for students to collaborate with them on academic projects. For example, take Emma Seguin, who we met in the last chapter. CNU professor Dr. Ron Sheffield recently co-authored a scholarly book, *Native American Entrepreneurs*, regarding the challenges and opportunities faced by Native American entrepreneurs. A member of the Quechan Tribe of Fort Yuma, Arizona, Dr. Sheffield teaches leadership courses at CNU.

"While starting a business can be daunting for anyone, indigenous people of North America have a unique set of challenges to overcome," Ron Sheffield says. But they are resilient. As one young Native American woman said, the main thing that kept her going is that you cannot "be afraid to fail. One thing I have learned about entrepreneurship is to dream big...you might not always succeed, but if you don't, you can always try again. I think it comes from growing up with parents who lived in poverty. They always told me that they knew what rock bottom looked like, and the worst that could happen was that they'd end up back there, but the best thing that could happen was that they would succeed."

Emma Seguin and nine other leadership students helped Dr. Sheffield interview 20 indigenous tribal members like this woman. As Ron wrote in his book's foreward, "Each of these brilliant students was chosen to assist with this rare research because of their natural ability to see the world as a place of opportunity, greatness, and never-ending compassion."

Dr. Jonathan White is a professor in Christopher Newport's American Studies program. He is also one of the nation's foremost scholars on Abraham Lincoln. He has written or edited 13 books—several that are prize-winning in Civil War historical circles—and more than a hundred articles, essays, and reviews about the Civil War.

Jonathan is also a Distinguished Lecturer for the Organization of American Historians, and serves on the Boards of Directors of the Abraham Lincoln Institute, the Abraham Lincoln Association, The Lincoln Forum, the Board of Advisors of the John L. Nau III Center for Civil War History at the University of Virginia, the Ford's Theatre Advisory Council, and the editorial board of the *Pennsylvania Magazine of History and Biography*. In 2019 he won the Outstanding Faculty Award of the State Council of Higher Education for Virginia, the highest award given to faculty members in the Commonwealth.

Jonathan has obviously received well-deserved recognition for his expertise and scholarship in his field. He's also the kind of guy who will dress up his tiny blonde daughters in Abe Lincoln stovepipe hats, or post creative, informative videos with his students, like one about the colorful role that whiskey played on the U.S.S. Monitor and other iron-clad ships in the late 19th century.

"I love research and writing," says Jonathan. "And it energizes me when I find talented students who are interested in history in the way that I am. I teach them to read 19th-century handwriting, and they get excited" as they explore original Civil War documents in the National Archives or other historical repositories Jonathan makes available to them.

Jonathan's 2017 book, *Midnight in America: Darkness, Sleep, and Dreams During the Civil War*, is an ambitious account of something many of us have just not thought about. What did Civil War-era soldiers, and their families, *dream* about during those four years of horrific conflict? What did their dreams reveal about their experiences of war, and what do those night-time visions of 19th century men and women in both the North and South reveal about the ordinary human experiences of that period?

Jonathan's book is refreshingly well-written, and despite its content, will not put you to sleep. He and seven student researchers unearthed about 400 significant dreams from letters and other 160-year-old papers. These provided the grist for the book's poignant stories and provocative analysis. (Jonathan acknowledges that those 400 dreams were a small sample, given the fact that scientists say that the average individual has about five dreams per night, or 1,825 per year... so if one wrote about all the dreams of all the Americans who lived through the Civil War, that would be roughly 230 billion dreams.)

Jonathan also regularly takes Christopher Newport students on summer academic research trips, such as a recent journey to South Carolina. They traveled to Beaufort, where the Union Army took control in 1861. White plantation owners had fled the area, leaving 10,000 slaves behind. These Black men and women had the opportunity—and tough challenge—to establish new lives. The students learned about White women who journeyed from the North to set up prototype schools so formerly enslaved adults and children could learn to read. The students visited the cemetery established in 1863 for the remains of Union soldiers killed in the area, including the brave men of the 54th Massachusetts, the first regiment made up of free African American soldiers, featured years ago in the movie, "Glory." The group went on to Charleston to tour Fort Sumter, and see the site of the old slave market, and newer destinations like Mother Emanuel Church. They also took in a minor league baseball game.

One of the most important aspects of Jonathan's teaching, besides the fact that he is fun, is that he makes history come alive. When he introduces students to Abraham Lincoln, for example, his first lecture focuses at length on Lincoln's early years: the devastating loss of his mother, as well as the deaths of a little brother and sister. The heartbreak of being head-over-heels in love with a young woman who then dies of typhoid fever at age 22. The painstaking, gritty pursuit of an education, the rejection and the losses...

"This was not a marble man, carved in stone, remotely resting in the majestic memorial that bears his name in Washington, D.C.," Jonathan will tell his students. "This is, at this point in his journey, a man in his twenties, not much older than many of you, who experienced love, loss, depression, the things we have all experienced. Keep that in mind as you read these historical documents: they are written by real people."

In an entirely different arena of undergraduate research, Christopher Newport physics professor Dr. Edward Brash leads a team of faculty and student researchers in studying the structure of protons. The group uses nearby Jefferson Lab's powerful accelerators to measure the properties of the proton—part of a global effort to reveal the structures of the fundamental particles of the universe.

"We involve undergraduates in our research in ways usually reserved for graduate students at other institutions," Edward says. "This way they can define and refine their academic and professional goals...they benefit from the mentorship we provide and go on to mentor other students along the way. The students who work with the nuclear physics group at Thomas Jefferson National Accelerator Facility work side by side with preeminent scientists and engineers from all over the world, and more importantly, they contribute in a crucial way to the work being done there."

Annie Cecil, a business administration major in the Luter School of Business with a double minor in civic engagement and social entrepreneurship, graduated from Christopher Newport in 2016. She created a case study of STIHL, the outdoor power equipment company, for future students taking courses in the Luter School of Business. Through her in-depth study of STIHL manufacturing plants in Virginia Beach and Germany, Annie helped develop lesson plans and class materials, and co-wrote an academic journal article.

"I knew participating in undergraduate research would be an excellent opportunity to try something new and expand my knowledge of sustainability practices. With my research, I wanted to give students the opportunity to learn more about sustainability and how it pertains to businesses, and then be able to apply it in a real-world context," says Annie.

INTERNSHIPS

Like undergraduate research, internships give students the opportunity to try on their academic and career interests to see if they fit. Often, students who do well end up working full time after graduation at the companies for which they interned. For their part, corporations love the opportunity to "audition" potential future employees. It's a win-win.

One such internship relationship is with Canon Virginia, which we'll discuss more in a later chapter. Because of former CNU rector Scott Millar's executive leadership role at Canon, as well as Paul Trible's friendship with Canon's former CEO, there have been many excellent ties between Christopher Newport and the digital giant, whose manufacturing plant, the largest in the western hemisphere, is right in Newport News.

Canon has made it clear that the company doesn't want its new engineers to be narrowly educated, with expertise only in math and science. The company wants engineers who excel in these disciplines, of course, but who are also grounded in a liberal arts and sciences curriculum, young people who know music, the arts, humanities, and politics, who know how to think and dream, who will bring innovation, imagination, and a commitment to the world beyond.

Canon looks for young women and men who embody one of the company's prevailing values: Kyosei. This is a sense of commitment to the world and environment around us all, or as the company says, the value of "all people, regardless of race, religion, or culture, harmoniously living and working together into the future."

And Canon finds those young people at Christopher Newport.

Like Gabby Beddard, a Christopher Newport electrical engineering major, who interned at Canon's Manufacturing Engineering Department, focusing on improving the company's efficiency in Automated Coupling: the removal of cartridge couplings with a mechanical device rather than an employee, saving on human resources.

Or Emily Stanisha, who graduated from Christopher Newport in 2021 as an electrical engineering and neuroscience major. During her Canon internship, Emily built a test rig to "quantify durability during deformation of a device," which sounds to non-engineers like she designed equipment to measure how long something would hold together when it was blown up.

Christopher Newport students serve in internships in all kinds of other fields. Like at the Thomas Jefferson National Accelerator Facility, where a student named Nii-Boi Quartey, a 2021 applied physics major with a minor in mathematics, interned to probe the nucleus of the atom, toward the end of improving efficiency of the particle accelerators at the world-renowned facility.

Or there's Sequoia Benhart, who graduated in 2021. She felt understandably intimidated on the first day of her internship at the Victim Services Unit of the Newport News commonwealth attorney's office.

She didn't feel qualified to address the complex and daunting needs of survivors of domestic violence. She felt she did not truly know enough about trauma to express real empathy and help for people in awful situations.

But she found that the training at Christopher Newport in her 'Social Work Practice' course served her well. The students had role-played different client scenarios. They had worked hard to develop skills like active listening, reflection and applying a strengths-based approach. "Once I started to view my interactions with survivors the same way," says Sequoia, "I felt much more confident in my ability to communicate effectively and to understand their experiences better.

"After all, we are all human beings who want to feel heard, supported and respected, and through my application of these skills, I feel that I was able to convey those feelings to these survivors."

Sequoia accompanied these women through their court experiences. She worked closely with the Commonwealth's Attorneys who prosecuted the cases. She served as an advocate for the survivors, so they felt that their voices were being heard throughout the court process.

She also contacted survivors of domestic violence within 24 hours of incidents involving law enforcement, providing a listening ear, reinforcing them in their right to press charges in the face of violence, and helping them to feel safe in the aftermath. She found herself interacting with young women the same age as herself. Her heart went out to them, particularly when some would go back to their abusive boyfriend or husband, repeating the sad cycle of domestic violence.

After long conversations with one young woman, Sequoia said, "The most valuable thing that I have learned at my internship, something that I could not have understood or prepared myself for on my first day, was that she is not the last person I will have that conversation with. I am not the last person who will try to explain why she deserves respect and safety, but if I can be the person to make one person feel supported and empowered enough to end the cycle, then I am doing my job as an advocate."

STUDY ABROAD

In today's globally flat world, international study during college is more important than it has ever been.

A quick search of upcoming short-term international study programs for the next academic year at Christopher Newport shows 15 opportunities to study everything from business to the arts to social justice, history, leadership, the environment, and something intriguing called 'Paths of Development in Mathematics and Physics at the Time of the French Revolution.' These programs take place in colorful countries as varied as Iceland, Australia, Fiji, Hungary, South Africa, Italy, France, Great Britain, the Czech Republic, Scotland, and the Bahamas.

"I am a huge believer in international travel for students," says Mark Reimer, the ebullient and durable music professor who has been at Christopher Newport since 1992. He often takes his strongest students to explore opportunities with like-minded professionals in other countries. "It creates a special kind of empathy," says Mark. "For example, we took students to Cyprus and Greece for a symposium. We've also gone to Estonia, Latvia, Lithuania, Germany, and the Netherlands. Now students have friends in those countries. And when they see breaking headlines about those parts of the world, they aren't just remote stories that don't touch the students' lives; they feel a connection with the people who live there."

Mark regularly puts together international symposia for emerging conductors. It's rare for undergraduates in this field—particularly women—to have such opportunities, but his most recent gathering in Estonia brought together 27 conductors from all over the world who were willing to spend three days with students from Christopher Newport (and other universities), sharing their craft and building relationships.

"It's incredible," says Mark. "Students can profit from being exposed to professionals from Brazil, Argentina, France, Germany, Italy, Finland, Norway—it creates something in them that they can gain no other way."

Lori Underwood, Dean of the College of Arts and Humanities, and Quentin Kidd, Dean of the College of Social Sciences, regularly take students abroad for an interdisciplinary honors course called 'The Good Society.' The course explores the fundamental ideas that shape human culture, with an emphasis on considering how one's own life will in fact contribute to the common good. It's open to students with a 3.5 GPA or above, and is held in the magical, cobblestoned, bell-ringing environs of Oxford University.

Peter Miller, a President's Leadership Program student who graduated in 2020, tried to capture the life-changing import of what the historical setting and the intellectual environment had meant for him. "Here we were, learning from the generations of discoverers who have gone before, using facilities people have been using for centuries, but to solve the most modern problems."

Students can also take a semester-long 12-credit course load in countries from Thailand to Costa Rica to Morocco to Japan to the Netherlands to South Korea to Spain.

Another showcase international study option is the semester abroad program in Scotland at the University of Glasgow, one of the premiere academic centers in the world. Christopher Newport sends different gifted and personable professors to teach this program each year. One such prof is Dr. Tatiana Rizova.

Tatiana is a slender, dark-haired woman with an air of natural grace and hospitality. She is fluent in her native Bulgarian, English,

Spanish, Russian, and Portuguese, and can get by in Croatian, Czech, Hungarian, Italian, and French. She can make you feel welcome in any language.

Tatiana arrived at Christopher Newport in 2008 with a fresh PhD in Political Science from UCLA and a master's in political science from the University of Wisconsin. She did undergraduate work in applied economics and political science at the American University in Bulgaria.

When Tatiana first came to Newport News from UCLA for her job interview, she says she immediately had such a "warm feeling. A sense of belonging and community. It was so different. People were incredibly welcoming. I felt like I really could live here."

She arrived for the 2008-2009 academic year, right in the middle of a severe hurricane season. This was just not something she'd experienced in Bulgaria, Wisconsin, or California. "Don't worry," said her colleague, Quentin Kidd. "If we have to evacuate, you're coming with me and my wife and the dogs. We're here for you!"

Colleagues gave Tatiana—who was single at the time—a car, furniture, meals, and friendship. "I felt so accepted and cared for, with plenty of shoulders to lean on," says Tatiana. "You just can't say that about most institutions."

Over the years since then, Tatiana has seen not only changes in her own life, but in the students she teaches. "Each year the academic caliber increases," she says, "and I am always awestruck by how socially conscientious the students are today. They are so aware of what is going on around them. They do a phenomenal job academically, and they also pay attention and care about human needs beyond our campus."

Tatiana took 22 such students to the University of Glasgow for the 2019 spring semester. They "went native" as much as possible, living in the residence halls, eating in the cafeteria, tasting haggis, and getting to know other students from all over the world. Tatiana taught a course in Scottish nationalism, taking students through Scotland's history, national identity, and the cultural forces at play in

Brexit, taking place in March 2019 and perhaps the most significant political event in Europe since the collapse of the Berlin Wall in 1989. Students read widely, wrote response papers, a journal, and a final project, and traveled with Tatiana to Hadrian's Wall and the Scottish Borders, Edinburgh, the Highlands and the Isle of Skye, the Theatre Royal of Glasgow, Loch Lomond, and Stirling Castle, as well as Loch Ness to get a glimpse of Nessie. If you look at Tatiana's impressive syllabus for that class, the most noteworthy aspect is what is listed at the end: her contact information and the address of her lodging in Glasgow. She didn't just keep office hours during the day, she was constantly available for students for whatever they needed to process during that semester far from home. "You develop a special relationship of trust when you're in a foreign environment," she says. "Students would show me their journals; I developed such a fondness for each one. I got to know their aspirations, what troubles them, what their hopes are."

Tatiana points to Christopher Newport's unique combination of strong, personal relationships and academic excellence. "From Day One, I felt like I was part of the CNU family," Tatiana says. "I'm just so happy to be walking to my office each morning. It doesn't feel like work. I get to learn new things and teach new things. I love to see the light in my students' eyes when an idea suddenly snaps into place in their minds.

"The other day Quentin Kidd and I were saying, 'we actually get paid to do this—being in such a creative job and being in this beautiful place that inspires us on a daily basis. I feel light on my feet when I am here."

It's a great description.

Another professor who is light on his feet is the peripatetic Dr. Kip Redick, who has probably logged about 100 million miles in his Birkenstocks since he arrived at Christopher Newport in 1991.

Back in the mists of the hallucinogenic early 1970s, Kip served in the Marines, was wounded, honorably discharged, and then went on a "spiritual quest" with his best friend. They gave away all their possessions except what could fit in their backpacks, and hiked the 2650-mile Pacific Crest Trail from California's border with Mexico to the Canadian border. After that jaunt, Kip traversed North America six times, and ended up living on the North Shore of Hawaii in a Laz-E-Boy recliner parked in a magical grove of ironwood trees.

Kip's physical journeys elicited a spiritual awakening. He eventually sensed that he should go to college, and through a variety of adventures ended up at Christopher Newport. After graduating, he moved on to get his masters and PhD. He returned to Christopher Newport to teach philosophy and religion in 1991, and has since served as department chair, president of the faculty senate, and in 2020 he received the Alumni Society Award for Excellence in Teaching and Mentoring.

Two decades ago, Kip knew of no other academician in the disciplines of philosophy or religion who was taking students on long-distance trips in the wilderness. The wonderful thing about Christopher Newport is that if something doesn't exist, you can make it up. So Kip began, as he says, to construct "a pedagogy based on my own research approach, phenomenology," which some of us must look up in order to understand.

The result of Kip's constructs was a May semester course, 'Pilgrimage on the Appalachian Trail' which he has taught every May since 2002. He has also led other classes on Mt. Rainier's Wonderland Trail, and taught a leadership seminar, 'Crucible in the Wilderness' on the challenging 100-Mile Wilderness trail that culminates on the summit of Maine's Mount Katahdin.

He has led study abroad programs at the University of Glasgow, Prague, Morocco, Greece, and Italy, but his signature course is the program he leads every other summer on the Camino de Santiago. This is the network of walking paths that lead to the shrine of Saint James in the cathedral of Santiago de Compostela in northwestern Spain. It's been a pilgrimage route since the 10th century, and is today a UNESCO World Heritage Site that attracts about 300,000 people a year.

Walking with "Hippie Kippy," as students lovingly call Dr. Redick, they bed down each night at inexpensive hostels in the quaint villages that dot the pilgrim trail. They get up at dawn and hike about 15 to 20 miles in a normal day, finishing by noon because of the intense heat of the Spanish sun. Kip conducts his academic classes each evening. The students forge friendships with one another and with fellow pilgrims from all over the world. They learn about other cultures. They participate in communal meals, walking to the market to buy fresh peppers, tomatoes, garlic, bread and cheeses, then chop vegetables and share stories with the people they meet, bonding over the insights human beings can gain when they get away from all media, schedules, and distractions. There is a sense of "flow," or mindfulness in the moment, a state of complete immersion in the activity of the present, free from any sense of ego or self-consciousness.

"When flow happens," Kip writes in academic publications about the experience, "the pilgrim's full attention is focused on the present moment...Walking flow shifts awareness beyond self-consciousness. I call this kenotic walking or walking self-emptying...an embodied dialogue wherein the 'phenomenological given' gives fully in the gap between itself as transcendent and the pilgrim's...lived experience."

"I don't think in terms of 'flow,'" says Paul Trible, who prefers tasseled loafers to Birkenstocks. "But I do know that our students learn incredibly important lessons about life out on the trail with Kip. They learn that yes, life is about far more than one's own experience and one's own advancement. The life of significance is about living in such a way that one focuses on *others*—on lifting them up, helping them, setting the good of the community above one's own self-interest."

CHAPTER 16

THE CORE

"If you are planning for a year, sow rice; if you
are planning for a decade, plant trees; if you
are planning for a lifetime, educate people."

— *CHINESE PROVERB*

Provost Dave Doughty is fond of telling parents and students about a fifth-century fellow named Martianus Minneus Felix Capella, who was not, as some of us might suppose, the founder of modern-day a capella groups. He was the father of the foundational concept of a classical liberal arts and science education.

Martianus Minneus Felix Capella came from a Roman province of Africa now known as Algeria. In a mixture of Latin prose and elaborately allusive verse, he wrote about the essentials for a proper education. He built on the classical Greek understanding of liberal arts—the "subjects of study proper to free persons."

Dave Doughty builds off of Mr. Capella and the Greeks, saying that liberal arts and science studies encompass the essentials of "what an educated citizen needs to know to take an active role in civic life." As listed by the American Council of Trustees and Alumni, there are seven academic topics that are essential to the general education of citizens. These core courses of study are offered—and required at Christopher Newport:

- Literature;
- Composition;
- Economics;
- Mathematics;
- Foreign language;
- Science;
- American history or government.

Some of us may think, well, of course, those are the basics. What's so unusual about requiring these classic, fundamental subjects?

At this writing, Christopher Newport is America's only public university that requires the Big Seven. This comprehensive approach to the liberal arts and sciences is not required at any other public college or university in the United States.

Traditionally, higher learning institutions in the U.S. served to prepare citizens to participate effectively in the civic, political, and economic spheres of America's republic. Students earnestly studied a tough general education curriculum as well as a major specialty suited to their passions and academic gifts. These would prepare the young person to be an informed and caring member of society who understood how to be civically engaged and contribute to the public good, as well as to succeed personally in the workplace.

In many of our nation's schools of higher learning, this model of academic excellence and notion of civic responsibility is no longer a priority. Studies show that most serious colleges and universities require students to at least take courses in writing composition and the natural sciences. But 82 percent do not require their students to take a course in U.S. government or history. Forty-two percent do not require a college-level mathematics course. Sixty-nine percent don't require the study of literature. Eighty-eight percent don't require intermediate-level foreign language courses. And 97 percent do not require a course in economics.

This discouraging information comes to us from the American Council of Trustees and Alumni (ACTA). ACTA is an independent, nonprofit organization, a unique network of alumni and trustees from nearly 1,300 institutions of higher learning. It promotes academic excellence, freedom, and accountability at America's colleges and universities, toward the end that the next generation receives an intellectually rich, superior college education at an affordable price.

Each year ACTA publishes a study posing the question, "What Will They Learn?" which grades more than 1100 colleges and universities according to their curriculum, graduation rates, and commitment to free speech. It's a tremendous resource for students and parents considering where to spend their higher education savings. It goes beyond the pretty pictures and the high-sounding rhetoric of the glossy college marketing materials. It gets to the heart of the matter: what wealth of knowledge and wisdom can a student actually absorb at this school?

Some well-known, painfully expensive schools get failing grades from ACTA. Some lesser known, more affordable institutions get As and Bs. Some colleges add course requirements to strengthen their curriculum and raise their ACTA grades over time. And out of the approximately 1100 schools evaluated, Christopher Newport University is one of only a handful of schools to receive a perfect score.

ACTA points out that the global workforce needs students who have this kind of well-rounded education, and today's employers express dissatisfaction in graduates' workforce readiness. The grads lack proficiency in the very skills demanded by the 21st century job market—the capacity to think critically, communicate clearly, and the perspective of a global worldview. [xvi]

A study by PayScale, and executive development firm Future Workplace, collected data from 76,000 businesses, and found that 60 percent of the companies polled said that new graduates lacked critical thinking skills and attention to detail. Forty-four percent cited deficiencies in writing skills, and 39 percent were dissatisfied with recent grads' public speaking skills.[xvii]

As legendary Apple co-founder Steve Jobs once put it, "It is in Apple's DNA that technology alone is not enough—it's technology married with liberal arts, married with the humanities, that yields us the results that make our heart sing."[xviii]

America needs employers whose hearts are singing.

Michael Poliakoff is an intensely educated American academic who serves as president of ACTA. Michael wrestled at Yale, graduating magna cum laude with a degree in classical studies. He then went on to attend the University of Oxford on a Rhodes Scholarship, where he earned *Class I Honours in Literae Humaniores*. He then earned his PhD in classical studies from the University of Michigan.

He is the type of person whose conversation routinely includes quotes from T. S. Eliot, lines from Aeschylus in the original Greek, and references to current culture-shaping books. He testifies before Congress on higher education policy, shows up on YouTube, and engages in media interviews with a courtly sort of humble grace.

Michael met Paul Trible in 2012 after ACTA released a report on 39 colleges and universities in Virginia. The report found that "in too many places, graduation rates were low, administrative bloat was high, and tuition was taking an ever-larger percentage of family income." The report warned that "certain trends—if ignored—would threaten to erode the Commonwealth's historic prominence in American higher education."[xix]

"Paul was one of the first college administrators who called on me after that report came out," Michael says. They became friends, like-minded visionaries with a drive to bring out the best in America's higher education.

One day they were walking together across Christopher Newport's campus, and Paul was greeting students. "I'm very used to 'the presidential wave,'" Michael says. College presidents wave and students nod, and everyone just keeps walking. "But Paul was greeting students by name. He'd stop and engage with them, asking about their families. He teased one student who was wearing a suit, 'Oh, you look so professional today!'

"It was amazing," Michael continues. "I have interns who work with me who went to smaller schools than Christopher Newport—often quite famous ones--and they'll tell me that they went to that school for four years and never even met the president personally. And here's CNU, 5,000 students, and Paul seemed to know them all."

On another day Michael was on Christopher Newport's campus and ran into Provost Dave Doughty, who had been interviewing potential professors. "What do you look for in faculty members?" Michael asked.

Dave told him, "I tell candidates, 'if you just want to come and do research, Christopher Newport is not the place for you. Or if you're only interested in teaching courses, this is not the right place. But if you want to engage your students, both inside and outside the classroom, then this is the place for you.'"

Despite Michael's expertise regarding colleges, when it came time for his daughter Moriah to apply to schools, he tried to rein himself in regarding his personal enthusiasm about Christopher Newport. Any parent will understand this dynamic: one must be prudent offering parental opinions to one's teenagers. Moriah visited CNU and liked it, but she'd also been accepted at a variety of prestigious schools. But, intrigued by Christopher Newport's American Studies program, she chose CNU.

She loved it.

One day Moriah called her father from Christopher Newport.

"Dad," she said, "did you ever read the Platonic dialogue called *The Theaetetus?*"

Well, because he's Michael Poliakoff, of course he had. In the Greek.

His daughter went on to tell him how wonderful her friends and classes were, and how her American studies professors, political scientist Dr. Nathan Busch and his wife Dr. Elizabeth Kaufer Busch—a prominent scholar in the field of American political thought and civic education—were hosting students for discussion groups at their home each week for discussion based on careful reading of Plato's *Dialogues*.

Wow, thought Michael, remembering Dave Doughty's comment about professors engaging their students in and out of the classroom. "Dave was not exaggerating."

"*This* is the kind of community CNU has built," Michael said later. "I could have borrowed a quarter-of-a-million dollars to send Moriah to some prominent school that flies on a prestigious reputation, and she never would have gotten the kind of education she did at CNU. CNU recognized her intellectual drive and provided the challenge and mentorship that she so wanted. She's still in touch with faculty there—those relationships have continued as she's gone on to further studies in graduate school at Boston College."

Too many colleges and universities today have splendid liberal arts mission statements, but fail to require their students to take a rigorous core curriculum. Students can bypass the majority of the seven core courses in favor of less demanding classes. As Michael points out, the "easy A" courses, "such as 'Science in Film,' 'American History through Baseball,' or 'History of Rock n' Roll in America' may be fun, and there may be a place for the odd niche course as a free elective... But as students often discover after they leave campus, they graduated without developing the intellectual abilities that would position them to excel in a competitive job market because their institution did not require them to take challenging courses that discipline and nourish the mind."

Michael augments this point by referencing a friend who says that when he takes his grandchildren to the grocery store, they don't tend to run toward the proteins and vegetables and whole grains. He must make sure that those nutritional essentials are in the cart. But too many schools have "set up a cafeteria line of cookies and candy, leaving students free to choose whatever they want. Their mission statements may be noble; they talk the talk, But they don't walk the walk."

He continues. "Christopher Newport walks the walk. It delivers on its promises."

THE HONORS PROGRAM

ACTA reports on the graduation rates of all the schools it surveys. One subset of Christopher Newport had a perfect 100 percent graduation rate in 2021, and that was the Honors Program. Interestingly, it may be the exception to CNU's core requirements, but as any Honors student will tell you, it is exceedingly rigorous.

The Honors program is a renewable scholarship designed for academically energetic students. Students with a high school GPA of at least 3.75 and an SAT score of at least 1310 in Evidence-Based Reading and Writing and Math may apply. One hundred or so are accepted each year. In 2021, those accepted students had an average high school GPA of 4.32, and an average SAT score of 1394. Their accelerated Honors seminar coursework satisfies Christopher Newport's liberal learning core requirements, with an added emphasis on CNU's pillars—service, study abroad, independent research, and internship opportunities. Working with honors advisors in their major disciplines, students can personalize academic plans that point toward their passions and professional aspirations.

It's not for everyone, but for curious, gifted students who know what they love, Honors at Christopher Newport is like a guided missile program that can challenge and equip them for strategic, powerful impact wherever they go.

Honors Program Director Dr. Jay Paul has been at Christopher Newport since 1978, when he arrived at the small commuter college to teach English. The Honors Program began in 1980 but went ballistic in its depth and excellence in 2008. Jay probably has more energy now than he did as a young man back in the '70s, simply because he loves interacting with Honors students. He serves as a sounding board, mentor, one-on-one advisor, provocateur, and guide as students explore their academic passions and engage with intellectual challenges that have important real-world implications.

Honors students wrestle with issues like economic disparities around the globe, the role of the United States in a turbulent world, the problem of evil as it plays out in issues like human trafficking, inequities in the cost of medicine, the role of propaganda during the French Revolution, and the essence of what it means to build a good society.

"I've been here for 45 years now," Jay says. "And since [the Honors Program started] it's just gotten better and better." If you have a cup of coffee with Jay, he'll remember student after student who graduated from the program. "Ah, yes, Elise; she went to Jordan after she graduated, studied Arabic, and taught little children in refugee camps for seven years. Then she fell in love..." Jay knows the whole story. There's Ben, who went to Johns Hopkins for medical school and is now an emergency room physician in Chicago...he married Nina, who went to Christopher Newport as well; she became an FBI agent... Casey, an English major who was a track star, went on to graduate school and now is a national officer for a venture capital initiative creating entrepreneurial opportunities in underserved areas. There's Jennifer, who went on to the University of Minnesota medical school and is now a professor at the Mayo Clinic.

The list goes on and on, and Jay smiles as he remembers each one, recalling how they learned to run with their strengths in the honors program at Christopher Newport, and then parlayed their learning to serve all kinds of people, with all kinds of needs, in a variety of real-world arenas.

STEM

We're all aware of the immense importance of science, technology, engineering, and math in today's global marketplace, and the great push to equip students from elementary school on up in these disciplines. As already noted, Christopher Newport combines its STEM excellence with a durable foundation in the humanities, producing well rounded citizen-students.

If you want to talk STEM at Christopher Newport, you go to Dave Doughty. He's an experimental physicist; STEM is his happy place. Over the course of his years at Christopher Newport, he's had a hand in developing a number of programs in applied physics, computer science, computer engineering, neuroscience, electrical engineering, cellular and molecular biology, biochemistry, and applied mathematics, to mention just a few. During his tenure as Dean of the College of Natural and Behavioral Sciences and later as university provost, the number of STEM majors doubled and the number of CNU students admitted to medical schools quadrupled.

Dave notes that education statistics have shifted dramatically. In 1951, four percent of adults had a college degree. When Dave graduated from college in 1970s, that number was 12 or 13 percent. Today about 35 percent of Americans graduate from college. "That's a monster minority," says Dave. To be competitive in the workplace, you must not only have an undergraduate degree, but that degree has to encompass far more than it used to. Dave tells any arts and humanities student who will listen, "Don't stop taking math until you get a C. He tells science-minded kids, "don't stop taking writing classes until you get a C." He tells everyone, "You can't just do the minimums. Employers and graduate schools are looking for the best."

The Canon family of companies has been a great fan of Christopher Newport for decades. This originated, says Scott Millar (former Christopher Newport rector, alumnus, and senior executive at Canon), at a dinner in Williamsburg back in 2005, when the company was celebrating 20 years of Canon's business growth in the Newport News area. Canon invited three speakers for their celebration: the mayor of Newport News, the governor of Virginia, and Paul Trible.

At the dinner before the program, Paul Trible was seated next to Yoroku Adachi, Canon USA's CEO at the time. "They really hit it off," Scott says. "Mr. Adachi's parents had been educators in Japan, and he and Paul found they had a lot in common."

That dinner discussion—which also focused on the importance of partnerships between Japan and America—led to a great friendship. Paul invited Mr. Adachi to continue the conversation with President's Leadership Program students at Christopher Newport, which included a number of STEM majors. Mr. Adachi got excited about the PLP, which we'll profile in the next chapter. He saw the tremendous potential for equipping generations of engineers who know how to lead. Paul—never shy about giving people an opportunity to invest their resources at Christopher Newport—asked Mr. Adachi if Canon would consider supporting the PLP. This led to a decade-long scholarship funding for the program.

Today, Canon Virginia has stepped up to provide financial support for outstanding electrical engineers, computer engineers and computer scientists who participate in Christopher Newport's President's Leadership Program. These students also receive the opportunity to intern onsite with Canon and engage with seasoned Canon engineers as their professional mentors.

"The remarkable transformation of Christopher Newport has been in large measure due to the extraordinary scholarship support from Canon," Paul Trible says about Christopher Newport's long friendship with Canon. "It is a natural fit for Canon Virginia and Christopher Newport to partner to both grow the local workforce and enrich the academic experience of our students."

"Over 30 percent of Christopher Newport students graduate in the STEM disciplines," says Dr. Nicole Guajardo, Dean of the College of Natural and Behavioral Sciences. And Canon's scholarship helps CNU "continue to recruit some of the strongest and most motivated students into our engineering and computer science programs."

Several years ago, when corporate giant Amazon announced its intentions to build a massive headquarters on the East Coast to complement its West Coast HQ, Virginia was a contender for this prize. Part of the Commonwealth's effort to lure the corporate giant was basically a human resources pitch. *Come to Virginia because of the excellence of our great universities and colleges. We'll invest over a billion dollars in our public institutions of higher learning to provide talent for you, steady crops of stellar STEM students for you to hire, since the majority of Amazon's employees work in information technology sectors of the company.*

For this and a hundred other great reasons, Amazon decided to locate its new headquarters in Arlington, Virginia. As part of the Commonwealth's deal with Amazon, Virginia announced a statewide Tech Talent Investment Program. This was a performance-based competition for state funding toward the goal that Virginia will produce 31,000 more college graduates in technology specialties by 2039.

In the fall of 2019, Christopher Newport was chosen to participate in the first round of funding of this important project; it was the only non-doctoral university chosen.

Dave Doughty, thrilled about Christopher Newport's growing STEM strength, as well as the fact that CNU beat out other higher ed contenders for the Tech Talent grant, sums it up well.

"I like to say, we punch above our weight class."

CHAPTER 17

LEADERSHIP

"If you ask people to give their very best,
they will astound you with their success."

— *PAUL TRIBLE*

"The President's Leadership Program was a fantastic way
to get immediately involved in the service community at
CNU, which helped me transform my skills in physics to
a pathway to really help people. The PLP helped me figure
out what a life of significance really looked like for me."

— *BROOK BYRD, CNU 2017*

F rom the beginning of Paul Trible's tenure at Christopher Newport, he has sought to make the university into a place that produces future leaders—young women and men richly educated in both mind and heart, equipped to step into the complexities of 21st century life and make a difference for good.

Sadly, in America in recent years, students have not always resonated with the notion of "leadership"; strident, divisive political office holders have tarnished young people's perspectives of what it means to be a leader.

That is why leading a life of service goes hand in hand with Christopher Newport's notion of leadership. It is a model of what's called servant leadership, in which the person out in front intentionally serves and humbly celebrates those who follow, and cares for and equips those who cannot yet care for themselves.

Christopher Newport's President's Leadership Program, or PLP, goes to the heart of what it means to prepare young women and men for a life of significance. It is not just an academic program focusing on the intellectual study of leadership concepts. It combines that academic analysis with experiential learning, personal development in accountability, and a strong work ethic. It equips students in their late teens and young twenties to know how to develop meaningful relationships, to engage in healthy (not endless) self-exploration and critical reflection, to become active citizens, to develop practical knowledge of leadership theories, and to discern how these play out in a constantly changing, challenging global society.

Established in 1998, the PLP became, as Paul Trible says, "the vehicle that has created the new Christopher Newport. It has helped us build the culture here. It has been a way to attract students of high academic quality and impart the kind of education of both minds and hearts that is so essential for young men and women to become people who live lives of significance."

The President's Leadership Program has evolved over the years, shaped by the expertise of Dr. Bob Colvin, a smooth, distinguished, and thoughtful leader. Bob is from Clifton Forge, Virginia; after college he worked in the criminal justice arena as a law enforcement officer, detective, and chief. He got his MBA, worked with the General Assembly in Richmond, and was appointed by then-Governor Doug Wilder to serve as Commissioner of the Commonwealth's Alcoholic Beverage Control Board, and then as Deputy Cabinet Secretary of Public Safety. During the term of the following governor, George Allen, Bob led the state Office of Consumer Affairs; he then got his PhD in executive leadership.

Bob knew of Paul Trible because of his involvement in Virginia politics. He came to Christopher Newport to teach political science in 1998, just before Christopher Newport launched its nascent leadership program. Over the following summer and fall, Bob wrote four detailed new leadership studies courses. Paul had read Bob's doctoral dissertation on executive leadership, and he was impressed. They worked together to strengthen the new PLP.

There was pushback from some faculty members, who felt that the university did not need an academic focus on leadership. Bob arranged for his mentor, James McGregor Burns, to come to campus for three days, along with leadership expert Georgia Sorenson. The late Dr. Burns was a Pulitzer-Prize winning author and one of the country's foremost scholars on leadership. He is credited with introducing the term "transforming leadership" to the field in his research on political leaders; the term soon spread to other realms, such as organizational psychology.

Dr. Burns and Dr. Sorenson held three days of public presentations, faculty meetings, and discussions with students. They reviewed the curriculum for Christopher Newport's leadership studies concentration, and publicly commended its design and content. They persuaded some skeptical faculty members of the rigor and legitimacy of this then-relatively new field of academic study.

"Nothing was going to stop Paul from establishing a nationally recognized, strong leadership program," Bob says. "His vision, his energy, and his positive outlook are contagious."

The PLP took hold, grew, and thrived. Paul's visionary urgency paid off.

"I'll tell you what working with Paul Trible is like," Bob continues. He describes a scene from when he worked in Governor Doug Wilder's office many years ago. He and the governor had just been discussing a project.

"How soon can you get that to me?" Governor Wilder asked.

Simultaneously, as Bob pulled out his calendar, the governor pushed up his sleeve to look at his watch.

"That's just like Paul," says Bob. "He wants it done today. Not tomorrow."

Today Bob Colvin serves as vice provost of undergraduate education. About 400 freshmen applicants are selected for the PLP every year. They tend to be students who have exhibited strong leadership characteristics in their high schools and communities. Recent PLP students had an average 4.0 high school GPA, and an average SAT score of 1301.

They can either double major or minor in leadership studies, and embark on a four-year program that leads them through courses in leadership theory, research, and writers like Plato, Aristotle, Machiavelli, Tolstoy, and the great religious leaders, who have all focused on the dynamics of leading and following.

Bob says that there's a common misconception that leaders are born, not made. But the principles of leadership *can* be learned, practiced, and mastered. Thirty years ago, people thought of leadership as achieving a position, but it's much more dispersed than that. Ethical leaders permeate every stratum and arena of society, and the PLP equips young people toward that end.

Students study leaders from George Washington to Chairman Mao to Nelson Mandela to Winston Churchill to Ellen Johnson Sirleaf, Nobel Peace Prize winner and two-term president of Liberia. They study the values that drive leadership, the distinctions between mission, vision, and values, and contrasts between leadership and management. They study cross-culture leadership, leadership in combat, leadership in times of peace. They study good leaders as well as bad leaders. Using rigorous, objective, scientific analysis, they find what really works.

As one PLP student emphasized this science behind his favorite course, 'Leadership Through the Ages' took the leadership theories we had learned in previous courses and applied it to consequential figures from John Adams and George Washington all the way to Juan and Eva Peron. Through the professor's instruction, I understood the science behind why and how those leaders made their decisions—both good and bad."

Like every program at Christopher Newport, the PLP's strongest asset is the relationships it fosters between professors and students.

A CNU graduate named Kenneth Kidd says that the PLP was a stunning program, but the best part of it was the relationships it built for him with two mentors in the Department of Leadership and American Studies.

"Dr. Sean Heuvel and Dr. Molly Waters took me under their collective wings when I was a freshman," Kenneth says. "They got to know me on a personal level outside of the classroom and helped me find a path during my undergraduate years that set me up for success and gave me opportunities that opened up so many doors." They connected Kenneth with his internships at Christopher Newport's Office of Alumni Relations, and with Fear2Freedom, a non-profit we'll look at in a later chapter. They also inspired him to get his Master's in Higher Education at William & Mary after he graduated from Christopher Newport. He now serves at CNU as Special Assistant to the President and aspires, no doubt, to one day be president of his alma mater.

Besides his many academic and business honors, Bob Colvin's distinguished tenure at Christopher Newport has brought him another great gift. A few years ago, Qingyan Tian, an educational leadership PhD from China's Gansu Province, arrived at Christopher Newport as a faculty member.

"I had felt the need for CNU to include more of a global perspective on what we were teaching," Bob says, "so I was excited: Tian had a lot of international experience and knew the leadership material inside and out."

As time went by, Bob and Tian often talked—at great length—about global issues, leadership theory, and everything in between...and eventually they realized they cared for one another. After clearing any conflict-of-interest issues because of their work relationship, they dated for several years, and then decided to marry.

Bob and Tian asked Paul Trible, a man of many abilities, to perform the ceremony. "He has been a mentor and a dear friend," Bob says. "We think the world of Paul and Rosemary, and since Tian and I had met at CNU, having Paul marry us seemed appropriate." The festive ceremony took place in the beautiful rotunda of Christopher Newport Hall.

Lest students start lining up to ask P. Tribs to conduct their own weddings, the administration kept the detail about the marriage officiant under wraps.

Until now.

Bob says that he loves his work at Christopher Newport, and he's proud of the enormous transformation that has taken place over the past 25 years. He tells about a friend, a fellow educator from a northern university who came to Christopher Newport. Bob showed him around.

"Bob," said his friend, "you've been to other public universities, right?"

Bob nodded.

"Well," the man continued. "They sure don't look like this."

It's true. Christopher Newport is a beautiful place. But it's not only its physical beauty that makes this community special. It's the urgent and infectious sense of mission, enthusiasm, and vision, as well as a buoyant sort of satisfaction, which drives the leaders there.

"The greatest thing about the PLP is that it doesn't just produce intelligent scholars and leaders, it produces scholars who want to make a difference for good in the world."

These are the words of a PhD candidate named Brook Byrd, who graduated from Christopher Newport in 2017. She's a stellar example of both the excellence and the social conscience of PLP students.

Brook's career thus far reads like an academic dream. She is both a Fulbright Scholar and a recipient of a Goldwater Scholarship, the most prestigious such honor in the U.S. for science and engineering undergraduates. She played on Christopher Newport's varsity tennis team, served as a volunteer high school swim coach, and graduated college with a perfect 4.0 GPA. She did an undergrad research internship at Harvard, got her master's in radiation therapy at England's University of Liverpool as a Fulbright Fellow, and went on to her PhD studies in health and medical physics at Dartmouth's Thayer School of Engineering.

"I knew I wanted to come to CNU and be involved in community service," Brook says. "I didn't know that academically it would lead me down this path. But, I'm the product of Christopher Newport's culture of developing students to reach for more, to change the world.

"The PLP is all about servant-leadership, which is serving the needs of others to impact the community in a way that raises their standards of life. I knew that's the leadership I wanted to pursue. I've been able to incorporate that in my physics to improve surgical outcomes and help breast cancer patients, as well as pursue research at the same time."

Even as Brook enjoys such honors, kudos, and success, the other thing that distinguishes her is her modesty. As her Christopher Newport physics professor Dr. David Heddle said about her, "She's this perfect storm of intelligence and curiosity and dedication and just pleasantness. [Sometimes] the best student in the class is not liked by the other students. It's a testament to her personality, that the other students all really love her."

As she works on her PhD at Dartmouth, Brook says, "It's not just about being 'smart' at CNU. It's about finding ways to make the world a better place, whether it's through science, or service, or both. After going to four different universities, I can definitely say that is a unique attribute of the CNU environment and the leaders it produces."

Students like Brook Byrd light Bob Colvin's heart on fire. "I could retire any day," he says. He could play endless rounds of golf, strum his banjo, and fly his Beechcraft Sundowner to scenic locations. "But I'm not working for money. I love Christopher Newport. I believe in this place. I get all kinds of messages from former students. Most of them end up with something like this: 'when the time came for me to step up and lead, I had everything I needed in my toolbox, because of my leadership studies courses.'"

CHAPTER 18

LOVE

"Lord, make me an instrument of Your peace. Where there
is hatred, let me sow love; where there is injury, pardon;
where there is doubt, faith; where there is despair, hope;
where there is darkness, light; where there is sadness, joy."

— *ST. FRANCIS OF ASSISI*

Any story about Christopher Newport's journey since 1996 would
not be complete without a focus on Rosemary Trible. She and
Paul have been a boxed set since 1971, and their partnership over the
years has had a natural grace to it, like skilled dancers who flow to the
music effortlessly, complementary, yet as one.

As has been said about the legendary dance duo Fred Astaire and
Ginger Rogers, "Yes, they were extraordinary. And Ginger did everything Fred did, but backwards and in high heels."

If you walk Christopher Newport's campus, Rosemary's contributions are evident everywhere, in every building. Because of her
experience as vice president of an international interior design firm,
she has served as a hard-working, unpaid collaborator at CNU, working with builders and designers to choose every paint color and sheen,
every chandelier and sconce, every piece of marble, every window

treatment and furniture style. Her aesthetic sense has made every campus building a place of inspiration and beauty.

From the beginning, Rosemary opened her home to everyone. Faculty, staff, administration, parents, students—all have been welcomed at gatherings of every sort that have taken place in her personal space, which is every bit as beautiful as the campus buildings she has decorated.

In keeping with Christopher Newport's priorities, the main group Rosemary welcomes to her home are students. Every first-year student comes to the Tribles during the first few weeks of school for peanut butter pie, and an introductory taste of CNU's signature hospitality.

For 25 years, Rosemary has hosted a weekly "Friends in Fellowship" gathering for female students, open to any and all who are interested. She loans out her dog for homesick students—they come over, pick up the dog and walk her on campus, where she is more popular than any homecoming queen. One day Paul Trible was walking between buildings, greeting everyone, and he spied a student strolling with a long leash, walking a beautiful golden retriever that looked familiar.

"Hi, Kate!" Paul called. "How are you? Do you have my dog?"

"Yes," the student replied. "But don't worry! I'll bring her home!"

One doubts that there is such easy rapport between the presidential couple and the students at most universities.

Rosemary's openness and love for students is also obvious at every graduation ceremony. As each gowned graduate exits the stage, diploma in hand, there is Rosemary, her arms wide open for the traditional Graduation Hug. She's usually on ice packs for a day or two after hugging over a thousand enthusiastic new graduates, but Rosemary's hugs—which are not reserved only for graduation—communicate the essence of Christopher Newport. This is a place where students matter, where each one is a valued part of the family.

But besides her considerable gifts of design, hospitality, and love, perhaps Rosemary's most significant legacy at Christopher Newport came from the most difficult experience in her life.

When she was 25, Rosemary and Paul had been married for four years. They lived in Tappahannock, Virginia, where Paul was a state prosecutor and pursuing a career in politics. Meanwhile, Rosemary's dream of working in broadcast communications had led to a live daytime television talk show in Richmond, Virginia. This was 1975, the concept was still in its infancy.

The show was called "Rosemary's Guest Book," and each weekday she interviewed all sorts of guests on topics of interest to women, her primary audience. Some shows focused on human interest stories, or design-oriented topics like a live tour of the Governor's Mansion, during which Rosemary interviewed the then-First Lady of Virginia.

Once a week, Rosemary focused on deeper issues. Just before Christmas 1975, she did a show that was gutsy for the times—she interviewed women who had been sexually assaulted, as well as a police officer and a prosecuting attorney. The victims' faces were in shadow on the set so they would not be identifiable, and Rosemary sensitively drew them out about their experiences, trying to bring a spotlight to a prevalent and terrible issue often left in the shadows back then.

The show generated a huge response, and Rosemary wept as she read letters and messages from women who up to that point had not been able to share their own grief and pain. They had felt completely alone. Until now.

A week or so later, Rosemary was taping several TV shows back-to-back so she could take time off with family back in Tappahannock during the Christmas holiday. She was staying alone at a hotel in downtown Richmond across the street from the television studio.

Working late on scripts for the next day, she found herself nodding off one evening. She went downstairs to the hotel restaurant to get a cup of coffee. When she returned to her room and turned to sit back down at the desk, she heard the curtains part behind her. She felt the cold steel of a gun at her temple, and a gloved hand around her throat. The man behind her bent down and hissed in her ear, "Okay, Cute Talk-Show Host. What do you do with a gun to your head?"

Rosemary, outweighed by at least 100 pounds, struggled, fought, wept, and prayed, but the assailant raped her, over and over. His rage, utter control over her, ski mask, and gloves made her feel like he had done this before. Many times.

Finally, he stood up. "I know who you are. I know where you live. And I promise I will kill you if you tell." Backing away, with the gun pointed toward her, he parted the curtains, then climbed out the window and dropped to the roof of the parking garage just below, disappearing into the darkness.

Rosemary immediately called the police, and Paul.

Her horrific experience stole her habitual trust in other people and her characteristic joie de vivre. Her assailant had left her in a prison of fear, even as she struggled to carry on with her public life. Paul did everything he could to comfort her, channeling his anger into aiding the police in their search for the perpetrator.

The authorities never found Rosemary's assailant. But over the years she came to a remarkable perspective about the awful crime. It was horrible, but it gave Rosemary the empathy and the tools to reach out to others whose lives had been ripped apart by sexual violence of all kinds. Her faith gave her the perspective that restored her joy. She believed that even though the attack had been horrifically evil, God could somehow use it for good in other people's lives, as well as her own.

Today's environment is very different than the tone of the times back in 1975. The #MeToo movement and other influencers have made sexual abuse of all kinds a much more public topic. Some stigmas are less strong, and more women—and men—report the crimes against them than in earlier times. Experts estimate that such crimes occur every 73 seconds in the U.S. The need is as great as ever, particularly on college campuses.

For years Rosemary has had a sixth sense for young people who have suffered abuse and sexual violence or harassment. She has created a safe haven of empathy and understanding, and students feel they can confide in her what they have told no one else. Young women have come to her and shared tears, hugs, and cups of tea. She has kept their confidences well.

In 2009 Rosemary wrote an account of her journey, *Fear to Freedom*, and in 2011 she founded Fear2Freedom, a non-profit organization dedicated to bringing dignity and hope to victims of sexual assault. F2F is designed to educate and sensitize university students and communities about sexual abuse. It helps college campuses create an atmosphere of zero tolerance toward sexual harassment and violence. It gives information and training about how to support survivors.

F2F also creates AfterCare and iCare kits. Victims of sexual assault who go to the hospital endure a PERK (physical evidence recovery kit) exam. Their personal belongings and all clothing are often collected as evidence for law enforcement. Already traumatized, the victims would often leave the hospital in hospital gowns, without personal hygiene items. F2F provides abused kids and adults with undergarments, a T-shirt, sweatpants, a toiletry kit, and a "freedom bear" to give a bit of furry comfort, along with a handwritten note of support from a student volunteer.

Thus far, more than 27,000 kits have been distributed to hospitals for survivors, and F2F's program was so well-received that it spread well beyond a partnership with Riverside Health System, which is down the street from Christopher Newport. F2F is active on 38 college and university campuses in 11 states at this writing, with 101 community partners and 44 hospital partners distributing F2F kits.[xx]

As one first-year student at Christopher Newport wrote to F2F, "Last year, I was raped in high school in Newport News. I went to Riverside for the PERK exam. I was in such trauma and when they presented me with this beautiful Fear 2 Freedom kit, I was really comforted. I want you to know I chose to come to CNU because of the compassion I received and the fact that you all have such a program. I was given hope, and now I love giving hope to others."

Like this brave young woman, many Christopher Newport's students choose to invest their service hours with F2F. Rosemary's influence at CNU—and many other universities—has indeed taken her personal trauma and used it for good.

Bobby Hatten, uber-successful attorney, rector of Christopher Newport, history buff, and one of the Tribles' oldest friends, is rarely at a loss for words, but he actually overflows when he talks about Rosemary Trible.

During the dedication of the Rosemary Trible Reading Room at the Christopher Newport library in 2018, Bobby compared Rosemary to Dolley Madison. Dolley was known in her day for her hospitality; she decorated the White House during James Madison's presidency.

She "carefully cultivated an image for the new nation," Bobby recounted during his speech at the dedication. "She chose paint colors—think of the Red Room, the Green Room, the Blue Room—as well as all the chairs, sofas, mirrors, carpets, tables, linens, plates, glasses, silverware and saltcellars. Her choices reflected the beauty and the values of the new republic.

"Tonight, we celebrate the gifts and life of our own...First Lady of Christopher Newport University: Rosemary Trible. Like Dolley Madison, she also married a Virginia lawyer who became a congressman, a senator and then a president (of CNU). Rosemary was critical in each of the lives she has shared with Paul.

"Rosemary Trible is the true heart of Christopher Newport University," Bobby continued in his poetic way.

"She is:
- the one who hugs every one of our students from the day they arrive until the day they graduate;
- the one who remembers your name;
- the one who is as comfortable and engaging with Supreme Court Justices as with football players;
- the one who constantly serves as a gracious host of elegant meals, receptions, and parties for alumni, Board members, faculty, families, and students in her home;
- the one who provides an example of moral leadership and courage to empower students and communities to combat sexual violence...

- the one who is largely responsible for CNU having one of the most beautiful campuses in America;
- and the one who, by Paul's own admission, has made him the man he is today."

Bobby's warm words on that cold December evening in 2018 could only be followed by a champagne toast and fireworks. So they were.

Around that same time, and in the months leading up to everyone's least favorite (because of Covid) year—2020—Rosemary struggled with increasingly difficult medical issues. She was her usual positive, energetic, and caring self, rarely complaining. But it was clear that she needed a season of medical care, rest, and recuperation.

In February 2021, Paul Trible made a short video for the Christopher Newport community. He announced that CNU's Board of Visitors had granted him a six-month sabbatical to care for his wife.

"Rosemary has been the joy and the love of my life for 50 years," Paul said. "She has supported me, encouraged me, and loved me unconditionally. She has shared my audacious dreams and aspirations and contributed decisively to all we have accomplished here at Christopher Newport, and all that has been accomplished in my now 50 years of public service."

"Now she needs me," Paul said simply. "And I need to be with Rosemary, to love and support and encourage her as she confronts and defeats a rare autoimmune disease that is sapping her muscle strength and making it increasingly difficult for her to walk and move and even breathe."

Paul went on to describe the aggressive series of intravenous infusions that doctors were hopeful could help Rosemary. Each monthly infusion, brimming with antibodies drawn from more than 1000 donors, would take five hours. The experts were hopeful that this regimen would help defeat the disease, and that Rosemary could move on to rebuild her remaining muscle through rigorous physical therapy. She also needed rest. Being still was uncharacteristic for the active Rosemary, but in this she was enthusiastically supported by the Tribles' new dog, an inky black lab with soulful eyes named Zoey, who was happy to recline at Rosemary's side at all times.

"I know these are challenging times for everyone," Paul continued. "I surely don't want to miss the final 11 weeks of classes [in the spring semester]. God knows I truly love this place."

He paused and took a breath.

"But there's no place and no person on this earth that I love more than Rosemary. I need to be with her. Now. And every step of the way. Every day, every hour, until she's able to regain her strength—as I know she will—and once again be able to run her usual 100 miles per hour, blessing every person she passes with her radiant smile and her loving, caring heart."

"So, thank you," Paul concluded, signing off with his signature line: "Go Captains!"

As soon as that video—short, simple, eloquent, and heartbreaking—went online, emails poured in. Cards, candy, flowers, fruit, balloons, and stuffed bears flooded the Tribles' front porch.

The Virginian-Pilot and The *Daily Press* called Rosemary "an indispensable partner and advocate" in an editorial about the inherent stresses in a "public service" marriage, noting that "The complexity of the demands...grow[s] significantly as one spouse gains rank and responsibility. The institutional obligations can be daunting, if not oppressive...It can break one direction or the other. It may work or it may not."

It worked.

"It's been perfectly obvious for a long time," the editorial continued. "Rosemary Trible did more than take in stride the ever-rising requirements of her partnership. She did more than justcooperate, did more than dutifully answer the call.

A fixture of the campus, a constant ally to the school's ambitions, Rosemary Trible also found the heart to detail a 1975 sexual assault and create...Fear2Freedom that helps sexual assault victims in their hour of crisis and aids their recovery. It is difficult, harrowing, and necessary work."[xxi]

The editorial noted that Paul had assured the Christopher Newport community that the university would be in good hands during the Tribles' sabbatical. "It has been all along," the writer concluded. "Due in no small measure to Rosemary Trible—the transcendent spouse."

Paul and his transcendent spouse returned to Christopher Newport in August 2021, as promised. (Christopher Newport had been beautifully led during his sabbatical by Chief of Staff Adelia Thompson and the rest of the CNU executive leadership team.) Rosemary will likely continue her super-infusions for the rest of her life, as well as deal with ongoing challenges to her health, though not to her well-being, which has been consistent throughout the journey. She and Paul returned to the university with their usual vigor, ebullience, and love.

The Tribles never could have known what their partnership—and Paul's strong decision to take a sabbatical to care for Rosemary rather than to simply hire caregivers and continue with his work—would mean for their legacy at Christopher Newport, about the heart and values of real servant-leadership.

CNU Vice Provost Bob Colvin has always said about Paul Trible, "Paul has the same, clear message that does not waiver. He lives it. The leader must wear the vision like a suit of clothes. He or she has to give people a reason why they would want to invest part of their lives in something you can do together that is greater than what any one of the team could have done on his own."

It's a great metaphor. And indeed, everything Paul has done over his years at Christopher Newport has shown his values, worn as consistently and comfortably as his suits and his tasseled loafers.

But the metaphor only goes so far, because even the greatest of leaders take off their fine clothes when they go home. In his decision to step away from Christopher Newport for a time because his wife was his top priority, Paul Trible showed generations of students, unforgettably, that the leader's true values are so central to his being that they apply both in the workplace with one's professional colleagues, and in the privacy of the home when the going gets tough. They are values not only worn like clothes, but values that are engraved on the heart.

CHAPTER 19

ENDINGS

"Life and leadership demand great dreams. We must not waste our lives on modest dreams. We must dream large and make our lives a great adventure. We must possess a loud and resounding 'yes' that will enable us to say no to all the distractions, doubters and naysayers. We must give our people a powerful purpose that will get them up early in the morning and allow them to sprint through the day. We were put on earth to make a contribution, to make a difference, to live a life of significance."

— *PAUL TRIBLE*

[Resumé virtues are] "the professional successes and accomplishments that one achieves in one's vocation....If a human being passes having only achieved material and professional success, but is not remembered with love for his or her service to others, then perhaps the tears are few, and the significance is hollow... [But] there are eulogy virtues—the good that one accomplished for others during one's lifetime. These acts of service are the things that people weep to remember, smiling through their tears, when one passes on."

— *DAVID BROOKS*

W hen Paul Trible took a sabbatical in 2021 to care for his wife, it wasn't the first time he made a vocational decision according to the values he holds most dear. So, it's worth taking a brief look further back in his story; it can inform our understanding of what "a life of significance" really means in the ongoing DNA of Christopher Newport University.

As you know, back in 1988 Paul was a young United States senator, a robust and rising political star. But he realized that the inherent demands of the Senate were, for him, at odds with the priority of his relationships with his wife, young son, and daughter.

He had had a rule ever since he was elected to Congress that he always wanted to be at home on Sundays to spend time with his family. His schedulers knew that if he was away for an event, he had to get home by Sunday.

"But even though I was physically present," Paul says, "I was mentally somewhere else. The Senate demands a total concentration of one's thoughts and energy. Though I had set that time apart for family, my kids knew that I wasn't really there. I was off saving western civilization, and I was missing actually living my life with Rosemary and the other people I loved the most."

He had entered the United States Senate with high hopes. Along with his fellow lawmakers on Capitol Hill, he was going to change the world, if not set it on fire.

But over time, he became increasingly frustrated with the glacial pace of the Congress...and the endless rhetoric and political posturing. It was surprisingly difficult to get important things done that would help actual people. This was in a day that was far more civil, and far less polarized, than the political atmosphere of our own challenging times.

A commitment to a life of public service can be a noble thing. But Paul came to believe that the future of the nation would not be shaped most powerfully by political forces, but by transformation in individual lives. He knew his calling was the same as it had always been, to serve, lead, love, and provide transformational impetus to a body of people for the common good. But he now knew that for him, at least, that calling could not be fulfilled in the slow-moving, and divided, United States Senate. As we've said, he had, in good faith, set his ladder against the wrong wall.

"I no longer wanted to be a United States senator. I didn't want to be president of the United States. I decided that was a life I did not want to lead, a sacrifice too great with rewards too slim."

He announced that he would not run again for the Senate. Understandably, many of his supporters were deeply disappointed. Some were angry. Rumors flew that he had a terminal disease. Some reporters traced his decision to his faith; perhaps he was going to go into the ministry or something. One journalist from a Richmond newspaper contacted Paul's mother to ask her about it. "Oh, Paul's not religious," she reassured him. "He's Episcopalian!"

Despite its stress, Paul's time in Congress produced some of the strongest relationships of his life. In 1977 he began meeting once a week in a hideaway office in the Capitol with a group of colleagues. They would have lunch, talk about the challenges they faced, and pray together about such things. These were individuals with quite different perspectives regarding the role and size of government and other political and ideological constructs.

But they came together as brothers on a common journey in life, supporting and encouraging one another. Sometimes their meetings would be interrupted by a call for a vote, and they'd have to rush to the floor of the Congress to cast their votes. Coming as they did from different ideological frameworks, they often voted differently. As Paul likes to say, "Yes, [Democrat] Don Bonker and I once figured out that we had canceled each other's votes out about 1200 times."

They had lunch once a week for 12 years, and significantly, their friendships continued after each of the four moved on to other things. Those relationships both shaped and reflected Paul's ability to find common ground with people who hold different points of view from his own. He's been quick, for years, to build friendships and allegiances with those who think differently.

Paul's capacity to do that stems from his faith, which nourishes a deep belief that every diverse human being is created in the image of God, with inherent rights, gifts, and dignity. That mindset underscores everything that Paul and Rosemary have sought to accomplish over their years at Christopher Newport University. Theirs is a faith that fuels a robust understanding of a vibrant civic square with true academic freedom, respect for all points of view, and a certain exhilaration of discovery in the journey of what it means to become a caring human being.

So, if that journey for Christopher Newport students begins with peanut butter pie, how does it end?

Graduation at CNU is always a glorious celebration. There are fireworks, hot air balloons, hugs, tears, speeches, toasts, bell ringing, parties, honors, and awards. It's a weekend whose intimacy, beauty, academic focus, and civic celebration reflects what students have learned over the previous four years.

It is the sweet-bitter closure of one season that leads into the next. Ninety-five percent of Christopher Newport students step right into full-time employment or graduate school. Other students enter the military, serve with relief agencies abroad, or engage in other service opportunities.

The rest of the Christopher Newport family—undergraduates and administrators and staff—smile through tears to see them go. Many faculty members, as we've seen, stay in touch with graduates over the years. Still, there are new young people to get to know, new students to equip for the journey. There are new-student orientations over the summer, short-term study abroad programs, courses to plan, and the ever-rising crop of high school juniors and seniors who arrive to tour CNU's campus.

So the cycle begins again, and the CNU story that commenced in 1996 with a professor proclaiming Trible "crazy as hell" hasn't turned out too badly after all.

Paul and Rosemary Trible have relished the thousands of extraordinary students who have been part of the Christopher Newport community for decades. And though the values, characteristics, and habits of the heart that define this special place will continue, Paul's long tenure at Christopher Newport will end in the summer of 2022. Every season must come to a close. But the legacy of his years there is as durable a supporting column for the school's architecture of the soul as its physical columns support its beautiful buildings.

Paul was indelibly reminded of this in the most intimate and surprising of ways when his father died.

Paul Trible Sr. was 87; he had lived a good, long life and then his body began to fail. He was in the hospital, but he wanted to go home to die.

Paul and Rosemary brought him to his family home overlooking the Chesapeake Bay in Northumberland County. They set him up in a room where he could gaze out his window from his hospital bed and see the waters he loved, beckoning on the horizon. His faithful dog, a big old Chesapeake Bay retriever named Ambrose, stayed by his side, sometimes carefully jumping up on the bed to lie next to his old friend.

Then the last day came. Paul and Rosemary held Mr. Trible's hands; Paul told his dad how much he loved him, reassuring him that he would love and care for his mother. All would be well. Mr. Trible took a last shallow breath and slipped away.

Rosemary had put the dog out of the room as Mr. Trible passed. But now Rosemary went out and got Ambrose, so the dog could, in his own way, say goodbye.

Ambrose had spent his days and nights under Mr. Trible's bed, jumping up and licking his hand, constantly attentive. Now he charged into the room, anxiously looking for Mr. Trible. He nosed the bed, looked under it, and jumped up to where Mr. Trible's body lay. He showed no recognition. He leapt down and raced around the room and out the door again, looking frantically for Mr. Trible. Where had he gone?

Ambrose somehow knew that human beings are more than just a material collection of chemicals in a suit of flesh. He's just a dog. But he knew that his beloved Mr. Trible Sr. was more than a body. He had a *soul*, and it was gone.

It seems that Christopher Newport's success over the years is tied, in a way, to what Ambrose the dog instinctively knew. The education of young human beings isn't just about material benefits like beautiful buildings, world-class facilities, rigorous intellectual challenges, and the absorption of complex information.

Yes, it's about educating the mind, of course, and that is done well at Christopher Newport. Students go on to all kinds of intellectual and professional successes. Writer David Brooks has called such achievements "resume virtues,"[xxii] and these are surely important.

But they are not paramount. One must begin with the end in mind. At the end of life, it is not the successes on our resumes, great as they are, that truly matter. The physical things, including this body within which we are housed, will pass, and they do not carry the essence of who we are.

One's purpose on this earth is more tied to realities that can't be seen through a microscope or charted on a spreadsheet or quantified in a lab. What matters is what David Brooks called the "eulogy virtues": love, selfless service for others, transformation of lives, and the viable good that is passed down to the next generation.

So the story of Christopher Newport University is not just about educating the mind toward the end of career success. It is more fundamentally about strengthening the virtues that remain: educating the heart and the soul, the most intrinsic part of what makes human beings able to desire, envision, and actually *live* a life of lasting significance.

Endings and new beginnings

A NOTE FROM THE AUTHOR

In the preceding pages, I wrote about grand notions like love being the secret sauce at CNU, its "culture of kindness," and the community's focus on relationships. I actually experienced all these things and more during the time that I researched and wrote this tome.

Sometimes when writers examine a person or institution up close, we can be disappointed. It's not that familiarity breeds contempt, which is a rather discouraging adage. It's just that sometimes beautiful things are not quite as delightful when one digs beneath their surface. I knew CNU moderately well. Our twins had spent four years there, and many other dear friends were graduates as well. I knew Paul and Rosemary Trible from a variety of shared adventures over the years. I had soulful relationships with each of their long line of distinguished dogs. I loved the Tribles and respected the school.

But as I researched the material for this book, I got to know CNU much better. I interviewed many members of the Christopher Newport community—faculty, administrators, students, alumni, community leaders, and neighbors. I talked with people who had experienced conflict at CNU. I heard about tough times. But I heard remarkably consistent stories about community, respect, commitment to a common good bigger than any one individual, and how conflicts can in fact produce stronger relationships and new solutions. I saw humor, energy, optimism, and pleasure—people loving what they do, using their gifts to give lift to the whole community.

I admire Paul's relentless vision about equipping students to live a life of significance, and the conscious way that that idea shaped every university-building detail during his tenure at Christopher Newport. I also appreciate his heart, which grows more and more tender with each passing year. I love Rosemary for her own ample love and consistent courage in the face of all kinds of adversities. I loved the administrators, staff, faculty, and friends of CNU who made themselves so generously available to me. Each one had such a distinct story, personality, and purpose, yet they all simmered with a common energy, good humor, enthusiasm, and deep love for their work and the students. These are people you want to go out with for a coffee or a beer, and they're also the kind of people you would want in your corner when the tough times come.

In terms of particulars, I'm grateful to Rosemary, Paul, and Zoey Trible for their warm hospitality. As always, I loved being the crazy aunt housed in their upstairs bedroom; the Tribles have always been organically gracious in sharing their lives and homes with me. Thank you to Eva Bland for your hospitality kindnesses to me as well! Thank you to everyone I interviewed, both named and unnamed, for this book. You were all so gracious with your time, insights, stories, and enthusiasm. Thank you to everyone in the president's office—Beverley Mueller, Sherry Crotts, and the relentlessly cheerful Kenneth Kidd—for innumerable cups of coffee and so many lovely lunches, for setting up interviews, giving me a great fake office in your board room, and digging up archives and resources. Thank you to Cindi Perry for your insights in reviewing the manuscript. Thank you to Bobby Hatten and Adelia Thompson for your time, wisdom, and expertise. Thank you to Amie Dale for quarterbacking the printing process, to Rachael Mitchell of Mitchell Freelance in Seattle for your editing wisdom, and to Jim Hanchett for your university communications help. Thank you to all who fact-checked so many intricate aspects of the manuscript; any errors that remain are entirely my own.

In today's environment, some critics will say that I interviewed the wrong people, or not enough of the right people, or that I did not capture *all* the voices of the university community. I hear you. But there is no such thing as the authoritative, exhaustive, impeccable, and universally approved version of any story. So this small book tells just one part of the ongoing tale of Christopher Newport...and I believe it's a story worth telling.

Ellen Vaughn
Reston, Virginia
February 2, 2022

ENDNOTES

[i] I am indebted to Dr. Phillip Hamilton's *Serving the Old Dominion: A History of Christopher Newport University*, 1958-2011 (Mercer University Press, Macon, Georgia, 2011) for well-rounded historcal details about Christopher Newport's early years.

[ii] Hamilton, p.111

[iii] Hamilton, p. 112

[iv] Hamilton, p. 114

[v] "Allen Names Trible Critic to CNU Board," Battinto Batts Jr., Daily Press, June 19, 1996, https://www.dailypress.com/news/dp-xpm-19960619-1996-06-19-9606190091-story.html

[vi] *USA Today*, Mike Jones, "Opinion: Tom Brady's Greatest Gift to the Buccaneers? Making Them Believe They Could Be Champions," February 8, 2021

[vii] Peter Felten, John N. Gardner, Charles C. Schroeder, Leo M. Lambert, Betsy O. Barefoot, *The Undergraduate Experience: Focusing Institutions on What Matters Most*, (San Francisco: Jossey-Bass, 2016), p. 7.

[viii] Daily Press, "$1 Million Donated for Arts Center," Kimberly Miller, May 8, 1998, https://www.dailypress.com/news/dp-xpm-19980508-1998-05-08-9805080106-story.html

[ix] *See Elevating the Human Spirit: The Architecture of Glavé & Holmes, 2019*

[x] "CNU's Trible Shakes up Staff—Again," Daily Press, Battinto Batts Jr., May 30, 1996, https://www.dailypress.com/news/dp-xpm-1996 0530-1996-05-30-9605300149-story.html

[xi] I am indebted to Jim Hanchett, CNU's Chief Communications Officer, for his abundant and diverse press releases about life at CNU.

[xii] "Letters to the Editor: Nice CNU Welcome," *Daily Press*, September 8, 1998, https://www.dailypress.com/news/dp-xpm-19980908-1998-09-08-9809080092-story.html

xiiiI am indebted to *The Undergraduate Experience: Focusing Institutions on What Matters Most,* by Peter Felten, John Gardner, Charles Schroeder, Leo Lambert, Betsy Barefoot, (Jossey-Bass, San Francisco, 2016), pages 100 – 103, for this synopsis of CNU's program.

xiv"New Community Captains Program Will Ease Local Students' Path to College," Jim Hanchett, November 27, 2018, https://cnu.edu/news/2018/11/28-cnu-comm_capts/#.YUo8_J1Kjcc

xv https://www.cbsnews.com/news/federal-regulators-plan-to-limit-speeds-of-large-trucks-and-buses/

xvi https://www.whatwilltheylearn.com/

xviihttps://www.cbsnews.com/news/employers-new-college-grads-arent-ready-for-workplace/

xviii https://www.wsj.com/articles/SB10001424053111190487540457 6532342684923826

xix https://www.goacta.org/resource/diffusion_of_light_and_education/

xx For more information, see https://www.fear2freedom.org/

xxiThe Virginian-Pilot & Daily Press editorial board, "For Rosemary Trible, an Indispensable Partner and Advocate," February 16, 2021, https://www.pilotonline.com/opinion/vp-ed-editorial-cnu-trible-0217-20210216-rfbgdbrewfechdbvvymqyjng54-story.html

xxii See https://www.nytimes.com/2015/04/12/opinion/sunday/david-brooks-the-moral-bucket-list.html

CPSIA information can be obtained
at www.ICGtesting.com
Printed in the USA
JSHW010810230423
40703JS00002B/8